MELVIN HANN was born and brought up in Bridport, and now lives in Dorchester. He joined the army in 1958 as an apprentice tradesman and served in such 'hotspots' as Harrogate, Chatham, Aldershot, Cyprus, Germany and Naples. After completing his nine years service in 1970 he was employed as the civilian 'plandrawer' at the Dorset and Bournemouth Constabulary Headquarters in Dorchester. His duties consisted of measuring and drawing scenes of crimes and fatal road traffic accidents as evidence to be produced in court. To fill the days he also provided for the graphical needs of the Winfrith Headquarters of Dorset Police. This post, especially after the advent of computers, has evolved into one of desktop publishing and computer graphics. A habit of keeping what others thought of as rubbish has enabled him to produce this book, his first attempt at writing.

FOLLOWING PAGE
The 'Green Arrows' entertaining the crowd at the Force Open Day in 1996.

BOBBIES ON THE BEAT
1856–2006

150 Years of the Dorset Police

MELVIN HANN

THE DOVECOTE PRESS

This is the attestation all new constables say and sign in front of a Justice of the Peace before taking up their appointment.

'I do solemnly and sincerely declare and affirm that I will well and truly serve the Queen in the office of Constable, with fairness, integrity, diligence and impartiality, upholding fundamental human rights and according equal respect to all people; and that I will, to the best of my power, cause the peace to be kept and preserved and prevent all offences against people and property; and that while I continue to hold the said office I will to the best of my skill and knowledge discharge all the duties thereof faithfully according to law.'

First published in 2006 by The Dovecote Press Ltd
Stanbridge, Wimborne Minster, Dorset BH21 4JD

ISBN 1 904349 45 5

© Dorset Police 2006

The author has asserted his rights under the Copyright, Designs
and Patent Act 1988 to be identified as author of this work

Designed by The Dovecote Press
Printed and bound in Singapore

All papers used by The Dovecote Press are natural, recyclable products
made from wood grown in sustainable, well-managed forests

A CIP catalogue record for this book is available
from the British Library

1 3 5 7 9 8 6 4 2

Contents

Foreword

THE CHIEF CONSTABLE OF DORSET POLICE
MARTIN BAKER QPM, BSc (Hons), MBA

Welcome to this marvellous celebration of the first 150 years of structured county-wide policing in Dorset. Skilfully written by Melvin Hann, this book celebrates the occasional tribulations and many achievements of the men and women who have served the people of Dorset over many generations in the incredibly varied, demanding and rewarding vocation that is policing.

Our communities and our workforce today are in some ways very different to those of the past. The communities we serve are ever more diverse in their composition and needs, while Dorset Police now comprises not only police officers but also many members of police staff (including our recently introduced Police Community Support Officers), the Special Constabulary – who themselves celebrate their 175th Anniversary this year – and many members of the public who have joined us as Volunteers to help us in our work. Without their essential support, contemporary police officers simply could not do their jobs.

While many of our current techniques, systems and technologies would be unrecognisable to our forebears, we share with them a recognition that there is one vital element necessary for good policing – the personal touch. By now implementing a system of dedicated neighbourhood policing in communities across Dorset, we believe we are bringing together the best of our past with the tools for the future.

In 2006 Dorset Police has two strategic objectives – To Make Dorset Safer; and, To Make Dorset Feel Safer. The role of the Dorset Police Authority in planning, resourcing and, on behalf of the public, scrutinising the work that we do is key to us achieving these objectives.

Of course, these objectives and our Values of Integrity, Professionalism, Fairness and Respect are not new; they are but a modern expression of the standards set by our predecessors. I am certain that they will be no less relevant to our successors 150 years hence. And their objectives, as with our own, will never be achieved by the police alone. Our partnerships with the people we serve and the many agencies with which we work have been and will remain vital to our success.

Irrespective of the future of Dorset Police as an organisation, people in Dorset will always need and deserve excellent policing and the highest quality service. I am both privileged and proud to lead and serve Dorset Police at this momentous time in its development and, as we strive to leave a legacy of A Safer Dorset for You, I commend to you this story of our heritage.

Martin Baker

ONE
'Charlies' and Constables

S PARE A THOUGHT for John Gould, the long-suffering parish constable of Upwey, near Weymouth. In 1625 he was forced to endure insults from a group of armed men as they spilled out from an alehouse, who after 'beating their breeches bid him come and kiss their tayles'. Undoubtedly the worse for wear, they finally ran off, 'holding their hatts upon their staves and whooping and hollering' – leaving Gould watching helplessly.

Nearly 400 years may have passed, but few Dorset police officers on duty at closing time today wouldn't recognise John Gould's predicament. For the modern police officer setting out on foot patrol today is following in the steps of the constables and watchmen once appointed to maintain law and order in Dorset's towns. Similarly, the high speed chase is not that far removed from the medieval 'hue and cry', when folk galloped off in pursuit of anyone they thought guilty of a crime.

Until the setting up of the Dorset Constabulary 150 years ago in 1856 there was no county wide professional police force. Policing was largely restricted to the boroughs. Much of rural Dorset belonged to large landowners, the squirearchy, whose stewards, estate managers and gamekeepers often acted as a private police force. The criminal law was maintained by the Justices of the Peace, acting under the county sheriff, and they appointed the constables and watchmen.

Watchmen, known as 'Charlies', originated from the reign of Charles II and were so badly paid that only the old and those unfit to do anything else were employed. They carried a bell, lantern, rattle and a staff and as watchmen were effective but as lawkeepers were largely useless. Beaminster's parish accounts for 1831 include the payment of 18 shillings for 'making two Great Coats with flaps & Capes for the Watchmen'. Constables were still overwhelmingly the unpaid men that had carried out the orders of the Justices of the Peace for centuries.

The most effective deterrent to committing a crime was the severity of the punishment if caught. A twelve-year-old gypsy girl caught picking a pocket in Wimborne was sentenced to a public flogging. Just occasionally an innocent man or woman was spared at the last moment, as in Beaminster in 1834 when a man called Crabb was on the verge of being flogged for the theft of a loaf of bread. Suddenly, someone in the watching crowd shouted out that it was he who had stolen the loaf. Chaos followed, and the flogging was abandoned for fear of a riot if it went ahead. Prior to a public whipping, usually 50 lashes on a bare back from a cat-o'-nine-tails, it was traditional to parade the prisoner round the town in a cart whilst the parish constable 'cried the sentence'.

At one stage 200 offences were punishable by death, including stealing a sheep or goods from a shop worth more than 25p. Blandford's last public execution was in 1741, when two men were hanged in the market place for robbery. Poole's was eleven years later, in 1742, when Anthony Colpis was hanged from the gallows on Baiter for throwing a widow from a third storey window. As a young man, the writer Thomas Hardy, watched the last public hanging of a woman in Dorchester in 1856, the year the Constabulary was established. A woman called Elizabeth Brown from Symondsbury had caught her husband making love to a local woman. Husband and wife later quarrelled. He attacked her with a whip, she retaliated with an axe, and a crowd of 4000 turned out in the drizzle of an August morning to watch her walk to the scaffold.

Much of the work of the constables and watchmen was spent dealing with more trivial offences – driving out vagrants, rounding up stray livestock, putting drunkards

The only surviving original lock-up in Dorset is behind the Swanage Town Hall and is inscribed 'Erected for the prevention of vice and immorality by the friends of religion and good order. 1803'.

and brawlers in the town stocks where they were pelted with rotten vegetables. Most towns had a pillory and ducking stool. Poole's ducking stool was on the Quay. Wimborne's stocks are still preserved in the garden of the Priest's House Museum. It was rough and ready justice, and served Dorset's needs at a time when there was a much stronger sense of community than today, and where most people spent their working lives in the towns and villages in which they were born. Poole had four constables. Blandford, Dorchester and Wimborne needed only two.

By the early nineteenth century it had become obvious that a more efficient police force was required. As in so many cases, it was rising crime in the capital that forced the government's hand. The seeds of the British police were sown in the eighteenth century during a period when two pints of gin could be bought for a penny. In London alone there were nearly 16,500 licensed premises. In some areas one in six houses could legally sell gin. Living conditions were appalling, with many eking out an existence in crowded slum tenements. Alcohol was an escape as well as a pleasure, but it did little to encourage a law abiding society. Organised criminal gangs ruled the poorer parts of the capital. Muggings were common, even on Pall Mall and in broad daylight.

The chief magistrate at Bow Street in Covent Garden was Henry Fielding, who as well as a lawyer was a writer. Ironically, Fielding has a link with Dorset, for he spent the early years of his marriage living a riotous life in East Stour, where he successfully spent his wife's fortune. She was a famous Salisbury beauty, and lives on as Sophie Weston, the heroine of Fielding's most celebrated novel, *Tom Jones*. By now sober and more sensible, Fielding concluded that to combat the rising crime rate in London a more efficient and organised body of constables was needed. In 1749 he recruited eight paid trustworthy constables to enforce the decisions of the magistrates in the area controlled from Bow Street.

The remarkable Sir John Fielding, born blind at birth, succeeded his stepbrother as the chief magistrate in 1754 and added a horse patrol of ten men to the little force, having first obtained a grant from the government, to tackle the highwaymen menacing the roads leading into London. The two men were undoubtedly London's two best eighteenth century magistrates. In a ballad of the period, a highwayman regrets going to London

'. . . one fine day
With my sweet love to see the play,
Where Fielding's gang did me pursue
And I was taken by that cursed crew.'

Sir John also introduced *The Weekly Pursuit*, a publication recording crimes and criminals, which later evolved into *The Police Gazette*. The patrols were a success and cleared the roads of highwaymen within a few months. The government then withdrew its funding, forcing the mounted patrol to be disbanded, leaving only the Bow Street Runners, whose ranks steadily grew.

The realisation that a regular paid police force was essential for the safety and welfare of the citizens was accepted in some important quarters. William Pitt introduced a Bill in 1785 to establish an adequate police force, but was compelled by public opinion to withdraw it, leaving individuals to take upon themselves the responsibility of maintaining law and order. In 1800 a paid body of 60 men was set up to police the River Thames in an effort to stop the large scale theft from the warehouses along the river, and five years later the Bow Street horse patrol was revived with a strength of 54 former cavalry troopers.

The belief in personal liberty, so important to the British, threatened all further attempts to create a national police force. The landowning gentry, from whose ranks came the majority of MPs, were suspicious of central government and anything that undermined their authority in the countryside. A parliamentary committee, appointed in 1822 to consider the merits of a paid police force, finally concluded:

'It is a practical impossibility to reconcile any effective system of policing with that perfect freedom of action and exception from interference which is one of the great privileges and blessings of society in this country. Your Committee think that the forfeiture or curtailment of such advantages would be too great a sacrifice for improvements in police or facilities in the detection of crime, however desirable in themselves if abstractly considered.'

During excessive displays of unruliness or riot the Yeomanry or army were called out. This could turn into tragedy, as in London in 1780 when the Gordon Riots led to 285 of the rioters being killed. The Gordon Riots began with a mob burning houses and four prisons, but what became known as the 'Peterloo Massacre' started as a peaceful meeting in Manchester in 1819 held to demand parliamentary reform, but the heavy-handedness of the Yeomanry left 11 dead, including two women, and about 400 wounded.

Peterloo was a symptom of the general unrest that

DORSET
ANY PERSON WILFULLY INJURING ANY PART OF THIS COUNTY BRIDGE • WILL BE GUILTY OF FELONY AND • UPON CONVICTION LIABLE TO BE TRANSPORTED FOR LIFE BY THE COURT
7&8 GEO 4 C30 S13 • T FOOKS

Signs like this were attached to many of the County's bridges in the early nineteenth century and give an indication of the harshness of the punishment at the time.

followed the Napoleonic Wars. Unemployment and low wages were commonplace – specially in the midland and northern cities spawned by the Industrial Revolution. The introduction of new textile machinery led to the rise of the Luddites, who deliberately set out to smash the machines that were taking their jobs. In 1830 it was the turn of the agricultural labourers of the south, Dorset included, whose frustration at their low wages and the threat posed by the introduction of threshing machinery exploded into violence. Ricks and barns were burnt, machines wrecked. There were no regular soldiers in Dorset so farmers and 'gentlemen' were sworn in as special constables, legalising their right to patrol the countryside. In Dorchester groups of armed men guarded the town at night. For over three weeks in November Sherborne's two watchmen were paid 1s 6d a night to sit up 'during the Riots'.

Four years later the Trade Union movement was born following the arrest of four Dorset labourers from the village of Tolpuddle for swearing a secret oath, again due to falling wages and rising unemployment. It fell to the parish constable to hand to his friend and neighbour, George Loveless, the warrant for his arrest. In his pamphlet, The Victims of Whiggery, Loveless later described the encounter: 'I arose to go to my usual labour, and had just left my house, when Mr James Brine, constable of the parish, met me and said, "I have a warrant for you, from the magistrates." "What is it's contents, Sir?" – "Take it yourself," said he, "you can read it as well as I can." – I did so. He asked, "Are you willing to go to the magistrates with me?" I answered, "To any place wherever you wish me." Accordingly I and my companions walked in company with the constable to Dorchester, about seven miles distant, and was taken into the house of a Mr Woolaston, magistrate, who, with his half brother James Frampton, and Edward Legg, were ready to receive us.'

The over-reaction of the Dorchester magistrates and harsh sentence imposed on the Tolpuddle Martyrs was in part inspired by fear brought on by the absence of an effective civilian police force. The use of the army to disperse rioters and guard machinery aggravated and made matters worse. It was against this background of civil unrest, or the threat of unrest, that in 1829, the Home Secretary, Sir Robert Peel, succeeded in passing through parliament the Metropolitan Police Act. The Act provided for a force of 300 paid constables to patrol an area within a 12 miles radius of Charing Cross. But even when established there was an air of apology about the need for a force: as if it wasn't quite the done thing. Their famous blue-coated uniform was designed to be recognisable but not to be military. Each constable was issued with a truncheon, but was instructed to keep it concealed in the tail pocket of his frock coat. Top hats were issued, reinforced with leather and embellished with the letter 'P'.

The booklet issued to each officer is one of the key documents in the history of the police, for it includes the following:

'It should be understood at the outset, that the object to be attained is the prevention of crime. The security of person and property, the preservation of the public tranquillity, and all the other objects of a police establishment will thus be better effected than by the detection and punishment of the offender after he has succeeded in committing the crime. Officers and police constables should endeavour to distinguish themselves by such vigilance and activity as may render it impossible for anyone to commit a crime within that portion of the town under their charge. The constable will be civil and obliging to all people of every rank and class'.

Thus did Peel lay down the principles for policing in this country: the prevention of crime, the protection of life and property, the preservation of the peace, and the insistence that police officers are the servants of the public.

Borough Forces

Sir Robert Peel's Act was extended beyond London's boundaries in 1835 when the Municipal Corporations Act was placed on the statute book. Under it, all boroughs subject to the act were required to provide a professional police force. Wimborne's last two parish constables, William Duffall and James Galpin, familiar sights in the town in their tall black hats and brass-buttoned coats, were replaced by a superintendent, sergeant and ten constables.

William Duffall, Wimborne's last parish constable.

Blandford's new force were all part-timers. The first superintendent was Francis Davis, who was paid £20 a year. His successor was a shopkeeper, the third a stocking and worsted maker, and the fourth was George Lanning, a dyer. As well as keeping the peace, they also collected tolls from the market. Their station was originally behind the Town Hall, but later they moved to Sheep Market Hill, next to the Library, where the words 'Borough Police' are still visible over the doorway.

A year after the first borough police forces had been established a Commission was set up to determine their effectiveness. Questionnaires were sent out asking for a report on the effects produced 'in respect of the prevention of crime and the general preservation of the peace and good order, by the appointment and action of a paid constabulary within your Borough'.

The reply of the Bridport Watch Committee provides a good illustration of a typical borough force. The town's superintendent and three constables policed an area of 600 acres, consisting of the parish of Bridport and parts of the parishes of Bradpole, Allington, Walditch, Burton Bradstock, Bothenhampton and Symondsbury – a combined population of 6,200. Their station house was on the east side of South Street and had two additional rooms for cells and lock ups. Each constable was issued with a greatcoat with a number marked on each side of the collar, a cape, and a tall hat with a case to keep it in. The uniforms cost £4. 5s for each officer. Superintendents were paid 16 shillings a week and constables 12 shillings a week from April to September and 14 shillings for the remainder of the year; the constables lived in their own homes at their own expense. It had cost £18 18s 10d to equip the police station and a further £2 5s 7d for stores, rattles, lanterns and lantern belts. Coal, candles and oil cost about £6 5s a year and uniforms £7 a year. Despite an extra £2 being paid by the Borough Council in compensation of wounds received in the execution of his duty by one constable, as well as a surgeon's bill of £1 9s, the Watch Committe confirmed that there were a 'reasonable number of sufficient men of good character and competent to serve as paid constables to be found.'

Most crucially, the authors of the report made it clear that the arrival of the force had reduced crime in Bridport and the surrounding area. 'There was increased quiet and order in the thick of night. Better order and regularity in the ale houses and beer houses. The more ready detection of offenders and nightly depradators, of great importance in a town where from the nature of trade, the manufacture of nets, twines and sailcloth, a vast deal of property is much reposed, and of characters difficult to identify. There are lodging houses for the reception of travellers, vagrants and trampers – such houses are no doubt the resort of thieves and habitual offenders.' The only concern was the 'numerous pickpockets and other thieves who go about the round of the county fairs, several were committed by the Borough Justices immediately after the Bridport Fair in October last but generally those committed are persons residing in the borough.'

The instructions for Bridport's police, like other boroughs in Dorset, were hand-written, and as well as setting out a list of possible crimes and misdeamenours tried to list them in order of gravity. 'Murder, housebreaking, robbery, stealing, picking pockets, receiving stolen goods knowing them to have been stolen, assaulting any one with intent to rob, setting fire to any church, house or other buildings, are some of the principle felonies – beside a great many more too numerous to be inserted here. Persons guilty of any of these offences are called felons.

'Smaller offences such as common assaults, affrays and riots are called misdemeanours. As it is most important to prevent and punish the commission of great crimes than of lesser offences, the constable has a greater power in cases of felonies than those in mere misdemeanours. But the first duty of a constable is always to prevent the commission of a crime.'

Similar forces were set up in the other Dorset boroughs. Weymouth's Police Force of 8 constables was established in 1846 under the command of an inspector: by the end of the century the force numbered over 30. Dorchester's numbers fluctuated slightly, but always consisted of a superintendent, a sergeant, and at least four constables, two of whom patrolled the town, and two Fordington. Initially the constables were issued with a stout walking

Helmet plate of the Dorchester Borough Police.

stick and a lantern. Their double-breasted coats bore the letter 'D' and the officer's number on either side of the collar. They had to enter the time they went on and off duty in a book, together with a report of any incidents, and the book was then taken to the town clerk's office every morning at 10 o'clock. In 1874 the number of constables was increased to six, on weekly wages of between 21 and 18 shillings. By then, the superintendent was taking home £100 a year and the sergeant a very precise £71 5 shillings and 8 pence.

Once the boroughs were professionally policed, criminals naturally found easier pickings in the Dorset countryside. To combat this the County Police Act of 1839, known as the 'Permissive Act', enabled Justices of the Peace in Quarter Sessions to appoint constables for rural areas if they thought existing arrangements were insufficient.

In the wake of the 'Permisive Act' police were established in the Sturminster, Shaftesbury and Wimborne Petty Sessional Divisions, and it was these officers who became the nucleus of the County Constabulary when, in 1856, the County and Borough Police Act was passed.

The Borough forces continued in tandem with the county force for various lengths of time before amalgamating with the county. Bridport, Lyme Regis and the Shaftesbury forces amalgamated in 1873, Wareham in 1887, Blandford and Dorchester in 1890, the Poole force the following year, but it was not until 1921 that Weymouth became the last borough force in the county to merge.

These little forces were not always popular. In Dorchester in 1864 in an effort to prevent the rowdy November 5th celebrations of previous years the practice of rolling lighted tar barrels down the High West and High East Streets was banned. Despite the ban, late in the evening a couple of flaming barrels were 'brought out by parties dressed in such grotesque costumes that no-one could identify them'. One of the borough police officers, P.C. Cozens, on duty that night, felled one of the men involved with such a blow that his police staff broke in two. The *Dorset County Chronicle* reported that 'the mob became infuriated, and the police had to beat a hasty retreat into the Town Hall.' Cozens was not the most popular of Dorchester's police – he had been burnt in effigy on the previous Guy Fawkes Night bonfire. Unfortunately, the road was being re-made outside the Town Hall. With a ready supply of stones so easily to hand the mob broke all the windows in the lower part of the Town Hall and in the Police Station in North Square. The *Dorset County Chronicle*'s account of the evening continues: 'To show the people's disapprobation of P.C. Cozens' unjustifiable attack on a harmless individual . . . an effigy, although of the most wretched description, was paraded through the streets followed by about 2,000 persons yelling and shouting – composed chiefly of females – to Maumbury Rings, where it was burnt.' Whatever his faults, P.C. Cozens deserves a little sympathy. A similar parade took place a few days later, except that his effigy was decapitated rather than burnt.

Dorchester Borough Police before their amalgamation with Dorset Constabulary in 1890.

Guy Fawkes Night in 1875 also caused a problem for the police in Dorchester, though it was very much of their own making. A constable was unwisely sent in plain clothes to try and buy '5s worth of fireworks from a person unlicensed to make such sales' and was of course recognised and ended up being chased through the town centre. The constable hid in an unlocked butcher's shop in High East Street but 'the mob pressed hard upon him, pelting mud and stones, and cried, "Turn him out, turn him out". Two of the windows were smashed, and the doors and shutters were battered.' Finally the enraged and innocent butcher emerged carrying an unloaded gun, but even so it took some time to disperse the crowd.

TWO

The County Constabulary

UNDER THE terms of the County and Borough Police Act of 1856 all counties throughout the British Isles were required to establish a properly organised police force under a Chief Constable for the rural areas and for those boroughs without a force. The Dorset Constabulary had been born.

The Police Committee, set up at the Midsummer Quarter Sessions that year, decided that the new County Constabulary's strength should consist of a Chief Constable, 3 Superintendents, 9 Inspectors, 9 Sergeants, 60 1st Class Constables and 30 2nd Class Constables.

Dorset's first Chief Constable was a 39-year-old ex-army officer from Beaminster, Lt Colonel Samuel Cox. The Colonel's first task was to recruit the new force, with the result that the following advertisement appeared in *The Dorset County Chronicle* on 17th November:

'The Magistrates of the County of Dorset having determined to establish a Rural Police Force throughout the County, and having done one the honour of appointing me Chief Constable, I am prepared to receive applications from all persons wishing to join the said force. All Applications must be accompanied by testimonials, addressed, prepaid, to Lt Colonel Cox, Chief Constable of Dorsetshire, Weymouth. The following will be the rates of pay: Superintendents, £130 per annum. Inspectors, £80 per annum, inclusive of clothing, both sets of Officers with allowance of £50 per annum for a Horse. Sergeants at £1 1s. per week, 1st Class Constables at 17/6d. per week and 2nd Class at 15/- exclusive of clothing. Except under Special circumstances, such as previous service in the police, no person will be appointed who is under 22 or over 35 years of age, or under 5ft 8ins in height, or who has more than two children dependent upon him for support. No candidate will be admitted who cannot write and read writing.
Samuel S. Cox, Chief Constable of Dorset.'

Colonel Cox decided against recruiting the 9 inspectors

Dorset's first Chief Constable, Lieutenant Colonel Samuel Symes Cox.

allotted to him, but chose instead to appoint ten superintendents, one of whom would be a Deputy Chief Constable and another a superintendent clerk. He issued his first General Order on 2nd December 1856, in which his primary concern was with the attitude he wished his men to adopt towards members of the public:

'A Constabulary Force being about to be raised for the County of Dorset, the Chief Constable trusts that he will have the zealous and active co-operation of all ranks, and that both Officers and men of the Establishment will contribute by every means in their power, to the well working of the Force and he hopes with their aid and assistance, to be enabled to establish a well organised Police throughout the County.

Poole Division in 1894 with bicycles and mascot. Note the moustaches, once officially ordered to be grown by all officers in the county.

The Chief Constable is desirous in the outset to impress upon every member of the Constabulary how very important it is on them to discharge their various duties with the utmost forbearance and perfect civility towards all classes and upon no occasion or under any provocation should they permit themselves to be rude or harsh in the performance of their Duty for nothing will serve more to create a kind feeling and cause the Force to be respected, and looked up to, than a conciliatory and decorous line of conduct.

The powers invested in them by law, they must exert with great caution and prudence and it is most essential that they keep under control, their private feelings.

The position in which the Constabulary Force is placed makes it particularly desirable that their conduct should be marked by civility and that they should show kindness and render assistance on all occasions when they see opportunities for so doing.'

He continued with an order that 'every Constable must be in his quarters at 10 o'clock at night, anyone seen out after that time will be reported to the Superintendent,' adding that officers in the force were to be 'particular' in having their hair cut and kept short. No such demands limited moustaches, of which every early photograph of a line of Dorset police boasts a remarkable array! Indeed, for

a while it was an official order that beards were forbidden throughout the force but that every officer was to grow a moustache.

When off duty, a constable had to return to his quarters after he had completed his duty to 'take the necessary rest' and to remain there until he went on duty again or was called out to deal with a specific matter. He was obliged to wear his uniform at all times, even to church, which he had to attend at least once on Sunday.

There was no weekly rest day or leave. The average day's duty, all of which had to be done on foot, was 12 hours, usually performed in two stints of about five hours' patrol during the day, and seven by night. A constable on patrol walked from 16 to 30 miles every day, much of that over unmetalled roads that in winter were a quagmire and in summer dusty. He was frequently expected to march prisoners by road to Dorchester Prison, and if he had to police fairs and other public gatherings, it sometimes meant leaving home at 3 a.m. in the morning, not returning until the early hours of the following day.

If an officer was informed of a 'Sudden Death or of a person Dying under circumstances of suspicion', he had to gather as much information as he could about the circumstances surrounding the death, then 'proceed without loss of time to report to his Superintendent, travelling at the rate of not less than three and a half miles an hour, unless he has the opportunity of coming more expeditiously by Rail.'

Every officer had to keep a journal and also had a pocket book. The entries by a Constable Hebditch, stationed in Cerne Abbas, between 1858 and 1861 give a good indication of the monotony of much of police work. The hours were long, the distances he covered considerable. The daily routine was enlivened from time to time by dealing with cases of petty larceny and summary offences, of which the most common was 'riding without reins'. Constable Hebditch visited public houses and farms on his beat and noted his weekly attendance at church on Sundays. He frequently walked from Cerne Abbas to Dorchester with prisoners, sometimes with as many as four at a time.

The long hours and lack of time off sometimes got the better of some newly recruited constables. The records show that in July 1857 a Constable Hodges felt inclined to 'spend several hours in a public house at Iwerne playing skittles, whilst there he had his pocket picked of his handcuffs by one of his companions, whom he took before a Magistrate, who, of course, immediately discharged him. The report continues: 'a more disreputable affair has not occurred since the Force has been established and the Chief Constable is determined to make an example of him. He is fined £1 and dismissed the force from this date. The Chief Constable wishes to take this opportunity of pointing out to the members of the Constabulary that no good can possibly arise from their entering public houses except in legitimate discharge of their duties, on the contrary some evil is sure to arise from it.'

The previous month Constable Rolls was fined ten shillings for 'laying down on the roadside when escorting a prisoner and allowing him to wander off out of his sight. The constable gives as a reason that the offence committed

Henry Paynes' certificate of service showing he had served from 1857 to 1861.

is a trivial one; this is no excuse, for had the prisoner escaped the same disgrace would have fallen on the constable and he would have been punished accordingly.'

A Wareham constable took out his pent up feelings on his equipment. He was 'reported for having damaged his lamp by kicking it on the Turnpike Road for upwards of half a mile between Wareham and Holme Bridge. Such a report the Chief Constable could hardly credit in the first instance, but it appears from enquiry that his lamp fell from his bundle and that the constable lost his temper and then acted in the most discreditable manner. He is perfectly unworthy to hold the position of 1st Class Constable and it will be some time before he can reclaim his position as a good officer. He is reduced to 2nd Class Constable and will make good the damage done.'

The Stoke Abbott Murder

It was not all fines and dismissals, however, for the Chief Constable's general orders are interspersed with such entries as, 'The Chief Constable has much satisfaction in noticing that at the late investigation respecting the Stoke Abbott Murder in the Beaminster Division a vote of thanks by the Coroner and Jury composing the Inquest was passed for the manner in which the case was put up and the way

Dorset's Victorian police stations were architecturally very similar, as (above) at Wareham and (left) at Wimborne. Wareham's first station was in South Street, and has since been replaced by the one in Worgret Road. Wimborne's Poole Road station (which had a magistrate's court attached) was demolished in 1976 when the new station was built.

the evidence was brought before them. The conduct of PC 47 Lavender who received the first intimation of the murder (having been left in charge of the station during the temporary absence of the Superintendent) is worthy of much commendation, and also for the manner in which he followed up the whole affair and in apprehending the Prisoner.'

The 'Stoke Abbott Murder' of 1858 was a rather sad and tragic case. A 'demented' lad from the village called James Seale had murdered a young woman called Sarah Ann Guppy by cutting her throat with a razor, later returning and setting fire to her lonely cottage. His final fate was inevitable, and his hanging was the first public event the new Constabulary policed. Constable Hebditch's journal include an August 1858 entry in which he explains that he was not at his usual meeting points for two days in a row in consequence of being on duty at the execution of James Seale in Dorchester.

The Dorset County Chronicle of August 12th describes

how 'this wretched youth was executed over the lodge of Dorchester County Gaol on Tuesday morning last'. Public executions had for a number of years been performed over the lodge of the gaol because the 'new drop' required a more complicated apparatus than the old gallows. Formerly executions had been carried out at the gallows site at Maumbury Rings.

Dorchester Town Council decided to exclude the public from the prison grounds, although spectators could watch from the meadows. On the morning of the sentence the Chief Constable took control of the prison grounds with a body of about 30 police under Superintendents Everitt, Blake and Plummer. According to the report there was only a small crowd of 3,000 spectators, and: 'No untoward incident occurred except that a branch of a tree broke, precipitating a lad into the river. The crowd behaved on the whole with more than ordinary decorum, if we except that in one or two instances the police were pelted with clods and sticks.'

A Pint too Many

In 1862 the Police Committee reported that all the new police stations had been completed. The headquarters of the force had been in temporary accommodation behind the Shire Hall in Dorchester. Having had no success in purchasing Wollaston House in Durngate Street for a headquarters and a residence for the Chief Constable, a 'desirable site' in Fordington Field was acquired in 1858 from the Duchy of Cornwall for £180. The building built on this site served as the Constabulary Headquarters until 1978 and is still used today as the Dorchester Police Station. The other new stations were at Beaminster, Blandford, Cerne Abbas, Cranborne, Sherborne,

Any meeting of policemen were called 'conference points'. This group shows the chief constable with the superintendents and sergeant major in 1865. Compare this with the photograph on page 97.

Sturminster Newton, Wareham, and Wimborne, all built at a total cost of £18,605 11s 5d.

In the same year an entry in the General Orders makes it clear that the safe movement of prisoners was a key role of the new Constabulary – though the following account from just before Christmas suggests that even police officers occasionally succumbed to temptation. A drunk prisoner called Jeremiah Fudge was brought into Headquarters by PC Collins. Fudge had originally been

A group of officers with the new blue serge uniforms issued to the force in 1867.

escorted from Sturminster Newton to Buckland Newton, where he was handed over to a PC Marsh. The two men went into the Royal Oak Inn and had a pint each. Marsh then escorted Fudge to Piddletrenthide, where he handed him into the custody of a PC Collins, who suggested the two men down two more pints each to recover from the three-and-a-half mile walk. Collins and Fudge then set out for Dorchester, again stopping for a final pint. The account concludes: 'Persons in custody are to be allowed ordinary refreshment on the march and nothing more, but it appears that the prisoner was regaled at nearly every public house he came to. PC Marsh is a young constable and as he appears to have acted under the orders of PC Collins he is severely reprimanded. PC Collins is dismissed the force. '

Traffic duty, even then, was not overlooked. *The Dorset County Chronicle* of April 1867 reported that 'William Coward was charged with allowing his horse and cart to remain on the highway in Blandford so as to obstruct the free passage of same. PC Hann stated that he was on duty in Salisbury Street between ten and eleven o'clock on the night of the 15th inst,. and saw the defendant's horse and cart standing in front of the Black Bear Inn. They were there more than an hour, and stood across the road so as to prevent the passage of vehicles.' Coward admitted the offence and was fined 10 shillings.

PC Hann had to deal with a rather more serious matter than an incorrectly parked horse and cart when stationed at Cranborne a few years later. *The Dorset County Chronicle* reported that at the Wimborne Petty Sessions in March 1871, James, John and George Zebedee, along with Joseph and George Bailey and Charles Head were charged with violently assaulting two police constables while in the course of their duty, and that five of them had tried to stop the police arresting James Zebedee for the non-payment of a £2 penalty. At the court, PC Hann, who 'still walked with difficulty and exhibited his left thumb almost bitten through', stated that together with another officer he had gone to the Cross Keys public house to serve the warrant on Zebedee. Zebedee was drunk and refused to leave the Cross Keys. A scuffle started. The other five defendents had joined in. One struck Hann. Another nearly bit his thumb off and kicked the other policeman over the eye, 'sending the poor fellow flying several yards across the road. The severity of the struggle may be imagined when we state that although the distance between the Cross Keys and the station was only 100 yards, the constables were three-quarters of an hour conveying their prisoners thither.' Hann had called for assistance, but though a crowd of about 100 watched the struggle, only one had rallied to their side, and he was nearly knocked out. Perhaps understandably, neither of the two policeman had been fit for duty since the attack.

The *Chronicle* went on to conclude, 'Lord Ashley said the whole of this disgraceful outrage resulted from drink. When sober James Zebedee was a quiet, civil, hardworking man, but when drunk he was the terror of the neighbourhood, and he only wondered that he had not added murder to his list of crimes. The Bench said that this was one of the most atrocious cases that had ever come before them. The police had exhibited remarkable courage and temper, for, although brutally assailed, they had not used their staves, and it was disgraceful that out of a hundred spectators only one man was found willing to assist. The Deputy Chief Constable produced a long list of convictions against most of the prisoners and the Bench sentenced each of them to six months hard labour.

Every rural beat officer was issued with a register in which he had to keep a record of bad or suspicious characters and of persons convicted before a magistrate. One of the original books, covering the period from 1858 to 1881 for the Sixpenny Handley beat, illustrates some of the offences and punishments of the time. At Wimborne in 1877, Charles Hains, aged 11, who had stolen three shillings from a shop, was punished by two hours in the police cells and six strokes of the birch rod.

Drunkenness and poaching were the most common offences and were dealt with no less harshly than offences

The birching stool and birch kept at the old Wimborne Police Station. The General Orders of the 1890s include an order that a second officer should be present when a boy was being birched.

we would consider today much more serious. For example, in 1879 Edward Cooke was fined £1 and costs for being drunk in charge of two horses and a waggon. The same month Henry Drake, a gypsy, was fined 10s and 30s costs for assault on police, and James Penny age 16, was fined 8s and 8s costs for poaching. In August William Upward was fined 5s with damages of 2s and costs of 9s for unlawfully releasing a horse from a pound, whereas in September John Wyatt, a woodman was fined 5s and 10s costs for beating a two year old child with a whip.

A Professional Force

Colonel Cox resigned as Chief Constable in 1867 and was replaced by Captain Amyatt Brown. To prepare himself for his new appointment, the Dublin-born Captain had some spent some time with the Metropolitan Police. He was 37 years old and had served with the 31st Regiment and later the 5th Lancers in the Crimea: sadly, no photograph of him is thought to have survived.

The new Chief Constable took command of a force that was now well established throughout Dorset and was settling into its routine duties – perhaps too routine, for following one of his early inspections, Brown issued an order stating that he had noticed the cells at some of the

A superintendent's horse and trap. The superintendent provided the horse and the Force provided the trap.

police stations were being used as lumber rooms. This practice, he said, must be discontinued forthwith, and he instructed that the cells and passages were to be cleared and whitewashed every April and October – an order faithfully observed until the 1940s.

To Captain Amyatt Brown we owe one of the glories of the Dorset Police, the remarkable 'Black Book' he wrote and issued to all constables, and which remained in use until the 1930s. It takes the form of a series of questions and answers, and the following examples hopefully give a flavour of the complete notebook

Q   If you saw a person about to commit a serious crime, what should you do?
A   Prevent it if possible, and apprehend him.
Q   How should a Constable carry out the orders of his superiors?
A   With cheerfulness and despatch.
Q   Name a few of the offences under the Highway Acts?
A   Riding without reins, allowing children under the age of 13 to have charge of a horse, not having a name on a cart, using an engine without having anything to screen it within 25 yards of the road, furious driving, Gypsies encamping by the side of the road, persons riding on Footpaths either with a horse, bicycle or tricycle.
Q   How should you walk when in charge of a prisoner?
A   On one side, about half a pace to the rear, so as to prevent him tripping me up.

When the Constabulary had originally been formed the county magistrates had suggested that all the towns accept the new force to police their boroughs. Only Shaftesbury had agreed, and the official notebook of PC James Searle still survives. PC Searle was stationed in the town from 1884 until he was moved to Piddlehinton the following year, principally because he had been visiting the house of a married woman. One of his first tasks had been to retrieve the corpse of a suicide from a pond in St James. Generally, his duties were fairly mundane: inspecting pubs, meeting trains at Semley, chasing escapees from the workhouse, and attending public occasions in the town. Like PC Hebditch at Cerne Abbas he was on his feet from dawn to dusk, walking immense mileages. He often escorted prisoners to Blandford on their way to Dorchester Prison, one week walking a total of 126 miles.

The zealous following of orders and being seen to be busy were initially sufficient for officers to gain promotion, but this changed with the introduction of exams in the 1870s. For constables these consisted of reading; writing neatly and correctly from dictation out of the Instruction Book; being able to add and subtract money; making out a sergeant's report and answering written questions as to a sergeant's general duties. If a constable was hesitant about putting his name forward to take the exams it was pointed out that 'the above amount of education is so simple that it cannot prevent any man who is otherwise fitted for the rank of sergeant from qualifying himself for promotion in a few weeks.'

For sergeants to be eligible for the rank of superintendent, they had to take a further exam in the following subjects: 'the multiplication and division of money, tables of weights and measures (superintendents had previously been made Inspectors of Weights and Measures); making out a superintendent's journal, pay, charge and summons sheet; classification of offences; answering written questions as to the duties of a superintendent and as to the general knowledge of the county, with the names of the principal towns and means of communication by railway and telegraph; and such a knowledge of drill as to be able to put a squad through the simplest movements of a company drill.'

Company drill was not neglected. There was a drill sergeant at headquarters where constables were periodically ordered to take a course of drill. The practise of taking examinations may have contributed to neat writing for it was reported that the 'Government Inspector had specially noticed the superior writing of the men of the Dorset Force as compared with those of other Counties in the District.'

Vagrancy and Victories

Dorset's police, in common with other forces, had to tackle a new problem arising from the large numbers of vagrants from outside the county who, sometimes in gangs, roamed the countryside through much of the late nineteenth century. So serious did the problem become that the superintendents ordered their officers to patrol by day in plain clothes, 'and to exert themselves to the utmost in apprehending all able-bodied Tramps who they may actually find begging or otherwise offending against the Law.'

These measures must have been successful because whereas at the Epiphany Sessions a half of the prisoners for trial were strangers to Dorset, at the next Quarter Sessions there was only one prisoner who was not from the county. Superintendent Eeles and his men at Wareham were commended for the excellent example they showed in an encounter with a gang of 16 tramps which had resulted in the arrest of all but five of them.

In May 1872 the Bath & West of England Society's Show was held at Dorchester. As this was one of the first large-scale operations undertaken by the County Constabulary, a force comprising the sergeant major, 5 sergeants and 35 constables under the command of the Deputy Chief Constable were used to police inside and outside the ground and to regulate the traffic as far as the borough boundary. Happily all went well, the Chief Constable being able to tell the force that he had great satisfaction in bringing to notice: 'the excellent manner in which the duties were carried out. Their conduct and appearance were a credit to the whole Force and were most favourably mentioned.'

This gave the Force the confidence to police the visit of the Prince of Wales when he visited Weymouth and Portland in August, despite the Chief Constable being urged to bring in the Metropolitan Police. Once again, the visit was successful, and the Force was rewarded with the personal thanks of the Prince of Wales, the Lords of the Admiralty and the Corporation of Weymouth.

Welfare

After two years in office, Chief Constable Brown announced that he was prepared to grant 7 days annual leave to any officer whose superintendent 'recommended the indulgence'. In 1873 he established a library of 'useful and entertaining books for the use of the members of the Force and their families'. The cost to the Force was scaled according to rank: superintendents four pence a month, sergeants three pence and constables two pence, the Chief Constable making a donation of £2 and promising £1 annually. A committee made up of all ranks was set up to select the books and to draw up the rules.

In the same year pay increases were introduced. The new scales ranged from £600 per annum for the Chief Constable down to 19s 10d a week for a 3rd class constable. By now the Constabularly had grown, and consisted of the Chief Constable, the deputy Chief Constable, 9 superintendents, one sergeant major, 22 sergeants and 114 constables.

The long winter hours on duty at night were gradually shortened to six. Some constables soon took took advantage of the reduction, for they had to be told that 'the night and other duties have been reduced as much as possible with a view to relieving them, but not with the view of their joining shooting parties or running after the hounds in uniform.' This last instruction is a reminder of how rural a county Dorset was. Few officers did not have some link with the land, and their status as keepers of the peace did not stop them playing a part in the county's rural traditions. Many a village policeman took his place amongst the guns for the end of season shoot on Dorset's farms and estates.

Although there were now far fewer charges of drinking and leaving the beat, the record still showed an occasional fall from grace. A convivial party at Cranborne police station resulted in the demotion of the sergeant to the bottom of the list of 1st Class Constables. He was reported for 'grossly transgressing one of the standing rules of the force by sending PC Melville to fetch 5 pints of beer and half a pint of gin for two prisoners who were in custody at Cranborne on a charge of drunkenness and disorderly

Bere Regis in about 1900, with two policemen on duty for the Woodbury Hill Fair.

conduct, and for also releasing the prisoners from the cells and drinking with them and the constables in his own quarters.'

A Murderous Assault

The only violent death of a serving police officer in Dorset so far occurred on the 20th September 1876 when Constable Thomas Bishop was assaulted at Bere Regis during the Woodbury Hill Fair. The last fair was held in the 1950s, when it was a pale shadow of its former self, but from Elizabethan times onwards the five day hill-top fair was the largest in Dorset, attracting traders from throughout the south. It was once notorious for the thieves, tricksters, pick-pockets and petty criminals it attracted, but by the 1870s the presence of the police had made it much safer.

Constable Bishop had been stationed at Bere Regis for over two years. At about 11 at night he was on duty with Constable Sansom, who had been temporarily posted to Bere Regis for the fair, when about 12 people came out of the Drax Arms, amongst whom was a 25 year old labourer called Henry Lock. A disturbance started, during which Lock was heard to mutter threats against Bishop, who had once summonsed him for being drunk and disorderly. The two officers advised the trouble makers to go quietly

This fine family photograph is of Constable 67 Stephen Stillman with his wife and children beside 'Uncle George's grave'. He joined in 1859 at Wareham and retired in 1885 on a pension of eighteen shillings per week.

home. Bishop took Lock by the arm and led him down a passageway to his house, whilst Constable Sansom kept the remainder at the entrance to the passage. Shortly afterwards, a neighbour, having seen Lock smashing Constable Bishop's head in with a chunk of flint, came running to Constable Sansom and told him to 'come quick as your mate is beaten bad'. Sansom rushed down the alley to find Bishop on the ground with his head battered in but still living. He took Bishop to his home where he died at 5.30 am the next morning. Sansom subsequently arrested Lock, who was later convicted of manslaughter and sentenced to a long term of imprisonment.

On the day of Constable Bishop's funeral all shops were shut in Bere Regis and blinds drawn in every house. A contingent of 24 constables, under the command of the Chief Constable, headed the funeral procession, followed by practically the entire population of the village. A fund for Constable Bishop's widow and eleven year old child was opened, which was started with a donation of £50. Chief Constable Brown later described Thomas Bishop as a man 'of most excellent character [who] died in the discharge of those duties which for 16 years he had carried out with credit to himself and to the County'.

Regrettably, no pension was paid to Thomas Bishop's widow. Instead, the Police Superannuation Fund granted her the highest gratuity possible, of just under £64. This paltry compensation for a husband and father was only

Weymouth Borough Police 1895.

£14 more than the first of the many donations to the fund. It was not until 14 years later that police widows became eligible for a pension on the death of their husband.

Commuting Criminals

By Victorian times the rapid development of the railway network had a considerable influence on crime, creating the need for co-ordination and closer co-operation between police forces. Already, in 1871, superintendents had been ordered to keep a register of convicted persons. If a stranger was taken into custody enquiries were then made to the Head Register Office (later the Criminal Record Office at New Scotland Yard) in London.

In 1880, a 'train watching' rota by officers in plain clothes was organised, following a spate of burglaries at country rectories throughout Dorset, Wiltshire and Somerset. Shaftesbury's James Searle's report book mentions donning plain clothes to watch the arrival of local trains. All trains were met and anyone looking suspicious was questioned or noted, and the results were so effective that the scheme was retained long after the original purpose had been served.

The keenness with which Constable John Matchum carried out his train watching in September 1884 won him the congratulations of the Chief Constable and promotion to acting sergeant. He had spotted two suspicious characters leave Upwey on an early train for London and although he had no information that any offence had been committed he sent a description to Superintendent Gale. The details of a robbery that had been committed at Portland the previous night had already been received by the superintendent and he was able to have the men arrested on the train when it stopped at Frome.

Inspectors

As the new county constabularies became more effective and their numbers increased, the government realised that the police provided a convenient and inexpensive agency for carrying out all manner of duties which other organisations were either unwilling or unable to undertake. In 1884 the Quarter Sessions sanctioned the employment of the police as assistant recruiting officers for the army and militia. Officers were asked to do all they could to encourage recruitment, but at the same time were reminded that on no account should they enter a public house for the purpose! A reward of 5/- for each army recruit and 2/6d. for each militia recruit was payable, half of which was paid into the Superannuation Fund. Recruits were either hard to find, or there was little encouragement to the constables from their superiors, for very few were recruited.

Superintendents and sergeants were also appointed as sampling officers for food and drugs, with additional duties under the Petroleum Act, the Explosives Act and the Contagious Diseases of Animals Act. It was not until 1953 that the police were relieved of all these unpaid 'Inspectorships'.

The Police Act of 1890 provided for pensions. Up until then small pensions or gratuities had occasionally been granted to officers who were found medically unfit, providing they had completed a substantial number of years' service; but no pension provision was made for an officer who retired normally upon the end of his service. The new Act provided a pension for a constable on completion of 26 years service, but officers above that rank had to wait until they reached 55 years of age, irrespective

Poole police before a bicycle race in Poole Park at the end of the nineteenth century.

of their years of service. Superintendent Lavender was the first officer to claim a pension under the new Police Act. Lavender was the officer who had arrested James Seale in 1858. By 1890 he had completed 34 years' service, 22 of them as a superintendent, and on retirement he became entitled to a well-earned pension of £112 10 shillings a year.

The same year that Superintendent Lavender went on duty for the final time three inspectors replaced the same number of 3rd class superintendents, thus marking the first mention of the rank of inspector in the Dorset Constabulary.

Bicycles

In 1894 the Dorchester Division was issued with just one bicycle. Evidently the experiment was successful, for the following year six more machines were purchased for use in other divisions. The arrival of the bicycle led to yet another of the endless minor instructions of which the police – despite their best intentions – are so fond: 'Whenever a Superintendent has occasion to send a constable on duty on a bicycle he must satisfy himself that the man is sufficiently a good rider to avoid the machine getting beyond his control.'

By 1896 an allowance of £3 a year was paid to officers for using their own machines. Bicycles were considered to be carriages within the meaning of the Highway Act. and had, therefore, to carry a lamp one hour after sunset to one hour before sunrise and also, 'upon overtaking any cart or carriage, horse, mule or other beast of burden or any foot passenger every such person shall within reasonable distance from and before passing sound a whistle or bell or give other audible and sufficient warning of their approach.'

BRING YOUR HEAD into . . JACKMAN'S
And we'll crown it   Next time you are in town,
for HALF-A-CROWN!   We keep going A-HEAD!!

OFFICIAL . . ⟩ Dorset . . .
                    Constabulary
PROGRAMME ⟩ Athletic . .
                    Club. . . .

Fourth Annual Sports,

RECREATION GROUND, DORCHESTER,

ON THURSDAY, JUNE 22, 1899,

Commencing at 2 p.m., sharp.

GYMNASTIC DISPLAY by a team from the Army Gymnastic Staff, under the direction of Staff-Sergt. Smith, at 3 p.m , 5 p.m., and 7 p.m.

TENT-PEGGING AND LEMON CUTTING,

Open to members of Q.O.D.Y.C. and N.C. Officers of the 73rd Field Battery R.A.
AT 4 p.m.

DANCING IN A SPACIOUS MARQUEE, AT 7.30.

It seems the traditionalist Chief Constable remained wary of this new means of transport, observing that 'on account of the many accidents that are constantly occurring the police cannot be too strict in enforcing the above regulations, especially as to warning foot passengers. Officers in charge of divisions will therefore pay particular attention to this matter and if necessary Constables will patrol the roads in plain clothes to put a stop to the dangerous practice of cyclists coming upon persons without warning.'

The menace of the bicycle may also have been responsible for the 1896 order that all policemen must undergo the St John Ambulance course. A year earlier, following the foundation of the Dorset Constabulary Athletics Club, the first Athletic Meeting was held in a modest way at Dorchester, and was so successful that it became an annual event for the following 63 years, with the exception of the years of the two World Wars.

By 1898 Captain Amyatt Brown had served for 31 years as Chief Constable. He too was entitled to enjoy the pension now paid to other officers on retirement. He was 68 and not well, and on 12th February he took his leave of the force he had done so much to help shape. Two months later, on the 16th April, 45 years old Captain Dennis Granville from Warwickshire took command of the Force. The Victorian age was about to come to a close, and a new century begin, ushering in challenges that few would have imagined when the first 90 constables took up their duties in Dorset nearly half a century earlier.

The Blandford Special Constabulary mobile unit was specially formed during the First World War, its members providing their own motorbikes.

THREE

The Force goes to War

The twentieth century began with a new Chief Constable in Captain Dennis Granville, a new monarch and with reform – in education, old age pensions, labour and in 1908 a Children's Act.

It wasn't reform so much as one day off a month that the constables and sergeants petitioned the Chief Constable for, who, although wanting to do what he could for the welfare of his men replied that he had to consider the interests of the ratepayers: 'The effect of granting this extra leave would mean that each man would have 22 days annual leave on full pay which is far in excess to that granted to any man in civil employment, in fact, in most trades it is "no work no pay".' He continued by saying he could not see 'how a man with a family can afford to take his family away for his annual leave and then spare money to be off either with or without his wife one day in every month.'

He did though grant additional leave of 21 days a year to superintendents, 14 days to sergeants, 13 days to 1st class constables (to be taken from April to September), 12 days to 2nd class constables (to be taken from February to March) and 11 days to 3rd class constables. The latter inevitably had the short end of the straw in that they were only allowed to take their leave during the winter months. In addition all ranks were permitted to take single days (to be deducted from their annual leave) and those involved in sport were allowed time off to play cricket or take part in the annual Athletics Meeting.

The Dorset Grey Uniform, Detectives and Tramps

In the spring of 1907 a new uniform was introduced for the summer months. It was made of a lightweight grey cloth and was far more comfortable than the thick blue serge – its other advantage being that it did not show the

Chief Constable Captain Dennis Granville.

ABOVE Chief Constable Granville with a body of his men. Note how his predecessor's order that every man should grow a moustache was still faithfully adhered to.

RIGHT Constable 116 Solomon Dennett modelling the Dorset Grey Uniform. He progressed and retired as a superintendent in 1915.

dust kicked up from the unmetalled roads. Unfortunately the Home Office did not appreciate the Dorset Constabulary's initiative and the experiment was abandoned in 1912.

The dusty roads of a Dorset summer were always a problem when it came to looking after uniforms. A constable serving in Bridport as late as 1922 commented that 'sometimes you couldn't see for the dust and your uniform would get in a hell of a mess.'

In the following year, 1908, the first detective was appointed. Although based at Dorchester, he was available to be called out by divisional superintendents throughout the county to assist with longer or more complicated investigations. Happily, serious crime was rare. The Force

Sherborne Division outside of the Sherborne Police Station just before the First World War. The notice on the wall to the right of the superintendent's head is advertising the Mendacity Society.

managed with just the one detective until 1921, and it took a further 14 years for a criminal investigation department to be established.

Dorset's only police detective probably did not have to concern himself with the age-old problem of tramps and wayfarers. In the years prior to the First World War the inhabitants of the county donated to a fund known as the Mendacity Society from which the police, who administered the fund, provided vouchers to needy vagrants for a free issue of bread and cheese. Mendacity Society posters were put up at shops where the vouchers could be exchanged, but as with all good intentions, the scheme did not always work out as expected and it was found that shopkeepers were exchanging the vouchers for tobacco. The Force took exception to this abuse of generosity and organised an undercover operation to catch out the offenders. A few officers were ordered to grow beards and, dressed as tramps, to present the mendacity vouchers at various shops.

The officer who thought of this scheme probably lived to regret it when the voucher system was withdrawn in

ABOVE Constable 72 Alfred Pride with his family at Buckland Newton Police Station in about 1907.

BELOW The Force tug-of-war team of 1913 won their contests at Dorchester, Weymouth and Taunton.

ABOVE The helmet plates worn between 1902 and 1935 on a sergeant's summer helmet, and a constable's helmet.

RIGHT The Dorset Wood Murder of March 1913 involved the death of Winifred Mitchell in Sovel's Wood near Gussage St Michael. William Burton, a married man, having thought he had got Winifred pregnant, lured her to the wood on the pretence of running away with her to London or Canada. He shot her and buried her body in a shallow grave that was later discovered. He was convicted of murder and hanged at Dorchester.

SUPPLEMENT TO LLOYD'S NEWS
·THE DORSET WOOD MURDER MYSTERY·

RELATIVES OF THE MURDERED GIRL LEAVING THE COURT

WILLIAM BURTON THE PRISONER

THE CROWD OUTSIDE THE COURT

WILLIAM WHITE AND HENRY PALMER THE TWO BOYS WHO FOUND THE GRAVE

MR MITCHAM & LEONARD MITCHAM

FREDERICK BUTT WHO GAVE EVIDENCE OF BURTONS STATEMENT THAT HE & THE GIRL INTENDED TO GO TO CANADA

A BUSH WHO GAVE EVIDENCE AS TO RELATIONS BETWEEN BURTON & MISS MITCHELL favour of issuing the bread and cheese from actual police stations. Large quantities of bread and cheese had to be bought on a daily basis, cut up, weighed, served and recorded. The bread consisted of a 2lb cottage loaf cut into four, whilst the skimmed milk cheese was commonly called chalk cheese because it was so hard. Some stations on the favoured vagrant routes were crowded to capacity with tramps waiting for or receiving their ration. Officers complained both of the dangers of disease and of the offence given to other members of the public calling at the stations, and it must have been a relief when this custom came to an end early in the First World War.

The Outbreak of War

The work of the police following the outbreak of the First World War in August 1914 continued as in peacetime but with added responsibilities. The specific war duties of the police were stated in a Home Office instruction as:

1. To increase police numbers to enable extra duties to be carried out.
2. To help with the mobilization of the army by displaying relevant posters and assisting with the prompt return of all reservists to their regiments.
3. To obtain billeting for officers, soldiers, and horses on the keepers of victualling houses and with full mobilization 'in public buildings, warehouses and private dwellings'.
4. Requisition of horses and vehicles. The police to explain to an owner who refuses to give up his horse or vehicle the national requirements, the law, and the compensation available. If the owner still refuses to take compulsory action as necessary.
5. Protection of vulnerable points, described as being from 'small bands of men provided with explosives who might do damage of such a nature as would delay mobilization.'
6. Espionage. To continue the precautions taken during peace to guard against espionage.
7. Control of undesirable aliens. 'A careful watch to be taken on aliens of the enemy's nationality visiting or residing in England, and also on undesirable aliens of whatever nationality because it will be from these classes that the persons are likely to be drawn who may commit outrages or act of espionage.'
8. Detention of enemy merchant ships. Although the Customs Officers took the necessary action to detain certain ships

A group of recruits with the sergeant drill instructor in 1908. Police drill instructors were loaned to the army during the First World War to teach drill.

belonging to, or carrying contraband of war for the enemy, they will require the protection of the police.
9. Watching of closed wireless stations. The police were required to report to the General Post Office any attempt to erect or replace aerial apparatus on premises from which they have been removed by the General Post Office and to report any installations observed on premises not mentioned in the lists furnished by the Post Office. To report any attempt to use portable wireless apparatus.
10. Construction of Defence Works. The police were to assist the military authorities if encroachment on private land to construct field defences was obstructed or delayed by the landowner.
11. Intelligence. 'Although it is not the specific task of the police to watch for the appearance or movement of ships of war or enemy aircraft, if a police officer is the first to observe the approach of enemy vessels he should inform the nearest military station or the headquarters of the Command'. It was noted that telegrams should, where possible, be supplemented by a telephone call, but discretion should be used in order that the telephone system be not congested.

Despite so lengthy a list of additional duties, the first task confronting the police was where to put interned

Austrians and Germans, as well as the anticipated prisoners of war. The Chief Constable suggested to the officer commanding Dorchester Barracks that they use the County School in Maud Road and the secondary schools in Bridport and Poole – all of which had well fenced playgrounds and could be easily guarded. He also proposed the site of Dorchester market, noting that the market would have to be suspended. In the event, part of the actual barracks were used to house foreign internees. Later the area below Poundbury was transformed into a prisoner of war camp, where up to 3,000 Germans were housed in lines of huts.

The additional officers joining the Constabulary placed a strain on police supplies. The Deputy Chief Constable had to admit to the superintendents that he lacked sufficient uniforms, suggesting that new recruits be issued with any spare uniforms hanging in officers' wardrobes and that they be allowed to wear helmets instead of caps. Another letter, to Superintendent Sprackling at Portland, informed the superintendent that once the purchase and mobilization of horses was complete he intended sending an officer to Abbotsbury with instructions to keep a close watch on the coastline and observe anyone who seemed to be acting suspiciously.

For a while, spies were presumed to be everywhere. Another constable was stationed at Swyre to maintain a watch on the Chesil. Two other officers, in plain clothes, were sent to keep a watch on the naval oil tanks at Portland, and two others the area surrounding the dockyard. Although there was a permanent military guard at the Whitehead torpedo factory at Wyke Regis three policemen, two from Shaftesbury, the third from Wimborne, were sent to Wyke Regis as an additional guard, whilst four more officers and a sergeant were posted to Grove Point and Portland Bill to guard the naval command posts controlling entry into Portland Harbour.

The early months of the war were marked by wild implausible rumours to which even the Chief Constable wasn't immune. It was he who brought to the attention of the local authority a report that attempts had been made by the enemy to introduce cholera germs into the water at Plymouth, Portsmouth and Aldershot. To make certain that nothing similar was attempted in Dorset, volunteers were enrolled to keep watch on all the local water supplies.

Shortly afterwards, the Chief Constable received a report from the Admiralty that a man representing himself as a scoutmaster, who spoke German, had been selling pills and liquor to sentries on duty. The report added that 'he was known to be a spy of a most dangerous character . . . He was fully armed, and a very sharp lookout should be kept for him and if found he should be arrested, but care taken that no opportunity was to be given him to use any weapon before he is disarmed.' Another report to reach the Chief Constable's desk was one from the War Office informing him that two foreigners had been caught in Cork, one selling pills and another scent sprays, both containing poison and disease germs. Both men had been shot.

The public's imagination sometimes got the better of it. Information was forwarded to Scotland Yard informing them that a German submarine base had been established in Pinhay Bay, near Lyme Regis. The only evidence for this was that a man found lying unconscious on the beach had stated, when he had regained consciousness, that someone had come up behind him and hit on the back of the head with a rock. It was immediately assumed it had been a German submariner who had come ashore, knocked the man out, and slipped back to his boat again. An old lady, also in Lyme, became convinced a man regularly seen near the same rocks was sending wireless messages to 'U' boats: he turned out to be a local man picking limpets. Further along the coast at Eype a patrol reported a figure at a lightened window night after night signalling out to sea. After much searching (according to the constable) he discovered the 'spy' was a young lady 'arranging her tresses before retiring to bed, oblivious of the fact she had not drawn the blind.'

Some constables were not quite as alert. A senior officer on his way back to Bridport from Lyme Regis decided to check on the special constables on duty at Seatown but was unable to find them. They were later discovered fast asleep in a homemade shelter with fish for their breakfast already prepared nearby: charitably, they were not woken, and lost only their breakfasts. It must be remembered that these men had probably done a day's work before being ordered to stay awake on a cold and lonely beach, and were expected to still be fit for duty on the following day.

Communications were still either basic or in the experimental stage. The Postmaster General had arranged with the London Wireless Society to forward to the police the names of those who could advise and assist them as to whether any particular apparatus found could be used for wireless telegraphy. Patrolling policeman, who were to look out for this equipment and had most likely never come across wireless equipment, were given help in Dorset by someone named as F. Cathery of Park View Studios in Parkstone.

Beacons and pigeons were still being used for communication. Beacons to be lit if any Germans landed or anything suspicious was spotted out to sea were sited at Lyme Regis, Chideock, West Bay, Abbotsbury, Lulworth, Gad Cliff and St Alban's Head. Of the 40 carrier pigeons stationed in Dorset there were six each at Lyme Regis, West Bay, Lulworth and St Alban's Head, with four at Wool, there were also six on the motor torpedo boat flotilla stationed off Portland and a further six on the Shambles Lightship. To help protect the pigeons a notice was published in local newspapers stating that 'It has been decided to use carrier pigeons for certain purposes in connection with His Majesty's Service. The public are therefore requested to refrain from shooting or otherwise interfering with carrier pigeons whilst on passage.' The Home Office requested the police should do their best to make known this direction.

The Lyme Regis imaginings were probably not influenced by alcohol, for even though Bridport and its surrounding villages were the only area in the county where the pre-war hours of licensing were retained, due to shortages the government had reduced the specific gravity of beer to such a degree that it was said to lack both body and strength. The severe food shortages led to other measures being taken to reduce waste. Sparrow and Rat Clubs were started in an attempt to reduce their numbers, whereby landowners, farmers and others paid into a club from which there was then a payout of 6d a dozen for rats, 2d a dozen for young sparrows and 1d per dozen for their

eggs. The police were required to enforce Food Orders: these ranged from dog licences and the prohibition of certain foods for anything other than human consumption to the careless adjustment of horses' nose-bags and resultant waste of feed.

Another duty that fell to the police was that of the 'prevention of the evils which may arise from the presence of women of immoral character in the neighbourhood of places where soldiers are quartered'. Although by 1914 some regional forces had recruited policewomen, Dorset was not one of them. To help, the Chief Constable enlisted the support of the 'National Union of Women Workers'. The Union's members were specially trained for their new duties, and each was given a card signed by the Chief Constable to show to any policemen when requesting help to do whatever was required to 'check prostitution and its evil consequences'.

War is not without tragedy. On New Year's Day 1915, the battleship HMS *Formidable* was struck by a torpedo some miles out from the Devon coast. It took an hour and a half to sink, and of the 750 crew only 233 were saved. One of the ship's cutters to survive the rough seas grounded at night on the beach in front of the Marine Parade in Lyme Regis in a raging storm. Despite the danger, the townspeople gathered on the beach and helped bring the survivors ashore. Although eight men and a boy were found dead in the bottom of the boat, the rest were carried through the surf, and taken into homes in the town. Among the rescuers was Sergeant J. Stockley who was awarded the Silver Medal of the Board of Trade for gallantry in saving life at sea and the Bronze Medallion of the Carnegie Hero Trust Fund, together with a cheque for £20 for his gallant conduct.

The loss of the *Formidable* has one unlikely footnote. Amongst those rescued and supposedly lying dead on the floor of the Pilot Boat Inn was an able seaman called John Cowan. It was only realized he was alive after he had been licked by the landlord's rough-haired collie, Lassie. The story reached Hollywood, inspiring the creation of the now immortal sheepdog that bears Lassie's name.

The Armistice was declared in November 1918, and the 51 officers who had been serving with the Colours rejoined

the Force at intervals over the next few months. The names of the constables who gave their lives are inscribed upon the War Memorial unveiled by the Lord Lieutenant, the Earl of Shaftesbury, on the 9th December 1920 outside the Constabulary Headquarters at Dorchester. Nine Dorset officers are listed: PC Albert Hill, Corporal, Iniskilling Fusiliers, killed in action in France; PC William Painter, Corporal, Dorset Regiment, died in hospital at Etaples, France; PC John Broomfield, Gunner, RGA, killed in action in France; PC Albert Hardy, private, Grenadier Guards, killed in action in France; PC Arthur Steel, sergeant, Dorset Regiment, died in hospital after service in France: PC Henry Hann, sergeant, Dorset Regiment, died in hospital in Baghdad; PC Joseph Cottrell, gunner, RGA, killed in action in Palestine; PC William Gale, private, Grenadier Guards, killed in action at Mons, PC James House, sergeant, Dorset Regiment, killed in action in Mesopotamia, and PC Stephen Reed, Coldstream Guards.

Of the others who served in the army PC Baigent and PC Ridout both rose to commissioned rank, PC Norris won the Military Medal, PCs Bowring and Park were awarded the Meritorious Service Medal and PC Loveless was mentioned in dispatches 'for gallant and distinguished service in the field'.

ABOVE The Lord Lieutenant, Lord Shaftesbury, unveiling the force war memorial in front of the Constabulary Headquarters in Dorchester in 1920.

BELOW Constable 53 Slow with Constable 14 Stephen Reed (on the right) who was one of those killed while serving in the army during the First World War.

FOUR

A Temporary Peace

Despite being granted a war bonus of up to 12 shillings a week for extra duties during the war there had been a steady deterioration in pay and allowances. Discontent led to the setting up of the National Union of Police and Prison Officers (NUPPO), and in 1918 the union called a police strike. Although well supported throughout the rest of the country the members in Dorset remained on duty. The government, stung into action by the strike, set up a committee under the chairmanship of Lord Desborough to examine police pay. The committee quickly reported and observed 'having regard to the nature of police work and the responsibilities . . . we consider the pay should not be assessed on the basis of that of an agricultural labourer or an unskilled worker, as has been the case.' There had been no national rates, it was very much up to Watch Committees as to what they paid. In Newcastle, for example, a constable was earning the same as a street sweeper.

The committee's findings were incorporated into the Police Act 1919 which doubled a constable's pay to £4 15s a week, abolished constable's gradings, and made it illegal for the police to join a trade union. Instead a Police Federation was created with Branch Boards in each force representing ranks up to inspector, its members being democratically elected.

Optimism and Depression

In Dorset the extra pay was welcome and may have resulted in a few additional brides. Before a constable got married he was required to not only obtain the Chief Constable's permission but to show he had at least £50 in savings. He was also expected to think carefully before hurrying into marriage, and to note the Chief Constable's

Constable 93 Harry Tom Lawrence in about 1920. The small leather pouch on his belt contained a first aid kit.

warning 'against forming friendships before taking the trouble to enquire whether such women were in every way respectable'.

This extra money did not last long. The post-war economy brought hardship and unemployment. There were thousands of demobbed servicemen, as well as widows and orphans. At the start of the 1920s the government needed to find savings and in 1922 a committee announced that money from the police budget could be saved by a reduction in pay of 2.5%, reducing the overall strength of the Force, the 'abolition of policewomen', and making cuts in rent and boot allowance.

In Dorset the strength remained at 265. There were no policewomen as yet, but the solitary civilian clerk was sacrificed. Additional money was saved by not issuing any new uniforms. The superintendents agreed to wear civilian clothes, thereby keeping their uniforms in the pristine condition expected of their rank.

The Police Pensions Act of 1921 made retirement compulsory at certain ages. For constables and sergeants this was to be on reaching the age of 55, inspectors and superintendents at 60, and assistant chief constables and chief constables at 65. Before receiving a full pension an officer was required to serve for 30 years (previously it had been 26 years) but for the first time there was to be pensions and allowances for the widows and children of policemen who had died.

Police work during this time is illustrated by the reminiscences of PC Tom Churchill, who retired in 1922 and later became the licensee of the Three Horseshoes in Burton Bradstock, recalling his days at Market Street Police Station in Poole.

On Saturday nights the tallest officers were detailed to do duty on the Quay, their principal task being to ensure that the crews of the many colliers and coasters tied up alongside behaved themselves and were safely back on board by 1am. Once fortified with a few drinks, a favourite sailors' occupation was to see how many policemen they could push over the edge of the Quay. It was usually the reverse that happened, a drunk sailor being no match for a well-built officer, and once in the water

Constable 133 Tom Churchill with his wife, Frances, and sons Alfred, who later joined the Salisbury City Constabulary, and James. Tom retired in 1922 and became the landlord of The Three Horseshoes in Burton Bradstock.

most sailors quickly sobered up and were hauled out by their crew mates. Once peace had returned, Poole's constables had to find the duty sergeant and inspector in order to get permission to return to the station. They were usually discovered somewhat the worse for wear, for the sergeant's and inspector's perks included downing the various pints which the landlords provided as a reward for keeping their pubs in order. Eventually a handcart was wheeled onto the Quay, onto which the sergeant and inspector were bundled before being pushed back to Market Street, where they were placed in the cells to sleep and sober up before the shift changeover at 6am.

Henry Sheldrake, who was a constable in Poole in the late 1920s remembered the cart as the only means of conveying drunk prisoners to the station. The magistrates in Poole had two courts at that time, one at the Guildhall, which sat every Thursday, and the other at Branksome. Any person arrested during the weekend would appear at Branksome Court and had to be taken there by public transport, usually on the electric tram that ran from Poole to Christchurch.

Superintendent Richard Hussey on his retirement in 1923. While a constable in Westham he made such an impression that when he left the inhabitants presented him with a handsome marble clock and silver teapot, which he was allowed to keep. While stationed at Broadmayne in 1897 he was treated less well. *The Dorset County Chronicle* reported: 'In September, 1897, a very unpleasant experience befell Mr Hussey and one which all but slit the thin-spun life. On the night of Woodbury Hill Fair a gang attacked him with savage brutality. The gang consisted of no less that 12 Poole Poachers who had reason to resent his vigilance and, to quote their own expression, meant to "put his light out".'

Dorset goes Motorised

The requisitioning of so many horses at the outbreak of war in 1914 led to a motorcycle and sidecar being hired for the superintendent's use at headquarters. The cost was £2 per week without the petrol, 100 gallons of which was bought at 1/6d per gallon. In the following year three 22hp Douglas motorcycles were purchased for the superin-

Captain Granville with his superintendents at a 'Conference Point' in February 1912.

tendent's use at Portland, Sturminster Newton and Wareham. Motorcars replaced all the horses in 1919 with the exception of the last remaining animal at Sherborne. In July 1922 the last horse in the Force was returned to the 'Military Authorities' and the Sherborne superintendent was given an allowance of £65 to use his own car. While some forces still have a mounted section, all traces of the horse in Dorset's police disappeared when the carts and harnesses were sold at auction in 1924.

The motorcar became a problem for the police just as the bicycle had been 30 years earlier. After one of the visits of the Prince of Wales to the county, the Chief Constable whilst praising those on duty for the way in which they had conducted themselves, noted that 'a few of the constables posted at dangerous corners or bends and crossroads failed to signal or warn an oncoming vehicle, the very reason for which they were posted at these places.'

Captain Granville, the Chief Constable, resigned in 1924, having held the post for 26 years. To mark his retirement he was presented with an array of gifts: the superintendents and inspectors gave a gold cigarette case, a malacca cane walking-stick embellished with a gold inscribed band as well as an address printed on vellum; the sergeants and constables a 'massive and handsome solid gold cigarette box lined with white satinwood – suitably engraved on the lid.' The Constabulary Athletic Club chipped in with a gold hunter watch and gave a Queen

The Force trumpeters play a fanfare for the Assizes Judge as he leaves his lodgings in Queen's Avenue, Dorchester. Circa 1920.

Chief Constable Major Lionel Peel Yates. He was a descendant of Sir Robert Peel, who in 1829 had created the first paid police force.

Anne silver tea service to Mrs Granville.

Major Lionel Westropp Peel Yates succeeded Captain Granville. Having previously served in the Royal Irish Constabulary, Dorset must have seemed a peaceful haven compared to Ireland and its 'Troubles'. Two years later though, in 1926, the General Strike intruded upon the peace. Although there were no disturbances in Dorset, a contingent was sent to the North Somerset Coalfield at Radstock in Somerset and another 55 men from the Force went to the Rhondda Valley in Glamorgan. It was the role of the police to escort the miners who wanted to work safely in and out of the pit, but naturally the striking miners did not take kindly to either the 'blacklegs' or to the police, showing their contempt by pelting them with rocks. Such behaviour came as a bit of a shock to officers used to the rural quiet of Dorset, and for many it was the first time they had to use their truncheons.

At the start of the strike the county was divided into two areas based upon Weymouth and Poole. Committees were formed and after appealing for volunteers to maintain essential services, 1,500 people came forward. Even more impressive were the 1,700 special constables sworn in, whose duties included guarding the railway sheds at Weymouth and controlling traffic. The *Dorset Daily Echo* reported that 'There have been no displays of temper and the splendid conduct of the strikers has helped everyone to keep as cheerful as possible.' The only known prosecution under the Emergency Regulations 1926 in the Weymouth area was of Frederick Legg, who in the bar of the Edward Hotel 'did an act calculated or likely to cause disaffection' by stating that two army regiments had joined the strike: he was later fined £2.

There were benefits to the police from the General Strike in that it united the service after divisions during the police strike and helped regain the respect of the public. So much so, that when the strike was over the *Times* launched a fund as a means of showing the nation's gratitude and collected nearly £250,000 in subscriptions. From this money the National Police Fund was established, which is still used today for welfare and recreational purposes.

The end of the General Strike was followed by recession and depression. Despite restrictions on spending, the Home Secretary urged the police to enforce the 1930 Road Traffic Act by mounting mobile patrols. The Force

The contingent of Dorset officers sent to Tonypandy during the coal strike of 1921.

complied and purchased eight Norton motorcycles, with the result that the first traffic police in Dorset made an appearance on its roads and lanes. Five years later they were joined by five motorcars, bought to replace worn out motorcycles at Blandford, Dorchester and Poole.

Throughout the decade the traffic on Dorset's roads steadily increased, and in 1938, when the Force's motorised fleet consisted of six patrol cars, six crime cars and seven motorcycles, a traffic department was set up with an inspector in charge, with a garage and workshop at Dorchester.

In the Cart

Jack and George Gray were brothers who had joined the Dorset Constabulary between the wars. Both men were liked and respected. George rose to the rank of superintendent and Jack to chief superintendent, the first in the Force. Jack Gray was a talented writer, and the following article he wrote for the Force newspaper many years later gives a good impression of police work in the 1930s. The conference points he mentions were the hourly

The first patrol motorcycles and riders pictured with the Chief Constable in front of the Dorchester Division offices. The machines were Norton 498cc OHV models with one for each of the eight divisions. The riders are PCs Bishop, Payne, Conway, Marsh, Culley, Stickley, Ward and Witt. In plus fours and tweed, the Chief Constable looks more like a country squire than a police officer!

meetings of the beat constable with his sergeant, there being no other means at that time for a constable to report anything untoward.

'In the early thirties, Wimborne did not have a sewage system and every night the lavatory buckets were collected by the night cart men. The night cart consisted of a large cylindrical tank on two wheels drawn by a horse. Into this tank the buckets were emptied by two heroes employed by the UDC. For the policemen on night duty the trick was to know which area was being served and to avoid it, as the stench was truly dreadful.

One night a young motorcyclist ran into the back of the cart and went head first into it. By the time I arrived, he had been pulled out of the cart, was seated on the footpath in agony (with a fractured kneecap) and kind folk from the nearby houses were trying to wash some of the mess off him. I made a figure of eight from some sheeting the neighbours brought out and applied it to his knee. This gave him considerable relief and quite unjustified faith in my ability.

Mr Rodway, the local garage owner and ambulance driver, arrived and with a good display of reluctant bravery loaded the injured man into the ambulance. I had to sit in the back with him and by the time we arrived at the Cottage Hospital, was just beginning to get a little used to the smell. Mr Rodway, too, was somewhat improved after a good throw-up. The night sister surprisingly behaved as if such an occasion was a regular feature, but I soon realised the reason for her apparent pleasure after she rang for the duty doctor. It was Doctor Le Flemyng, Chairman of the BMA and the leading proponent for the installation of mains sewerage. He was very interested in my figure of eight and asked me where I had learned how to do it. I told him at the British Red Cross and he said that he was a St John's man himself.

After the patient had been washed and treated, Dr Le Flemyng decided we had all better have an anti-tetanus injection, including himself. Sister enjoyed injecting all our rear ends until the doctor said "Come on Sister, in the office, it's your turn now".

'When this was all over I was just in time for my 3am conference point in the Square. Sergeant George Brickell was waiting by the telephone box and greeted me with "You're in the cart." "No, not me Sarge" I replied, thinking he must have heard of the night's happenings but he continued "the Super waited twenty minutes on your 1am point and you also missed

This extraordinary contraption was an illegel still, which was found on the premises of an ex-colonial police officer and used for making whisky that was sold to Bournemouth clubs. Constable Jack Gray is on the left with two Customs Officers.

supper". I realised then that he had no idea what had happened and tried to explain. "I bet you can", he snapped "but save it for the Super, report to him at 10am or you're on half a sheet". With that he jumped on his cycle and rode off. I had a good hour to ponder my dilemma and after I had made my 4am point I headed back to the station.

Superintendent 'Dodger' Day lived in the station and would often watch from behind his bedroom curtain to see that we did not come in too early. As I neared the station it was just beginning to break light and I could see his form standing behind the lace curtain. I went into the garden, stood under his window and offered my explanation but he did not acknowledge me and drew back into the room out of sight. I knew he had heard me because I heard Mrs Day ask "what's he talking about, Frank?" I went down to the charge room at 10am and Sid Jeans, the reserve man, asked me why I was not in bed. I told him I had to report to the Super at 10am. Sid then told me that neither the Super or the Sergeant were there and both had gone off for the day.

'The night duty was 7pm to 9pm and 10pm to 4am. That evening I was on duty in the Square when Dr Le Flemyng pulled up in his car to ask how the anti-tetanus was going. "Fine" I replied. He went on to tell me that he had rung my Superintendent first thing that morning to inform him about my figure of eight and what a help it had been to the casualty. The doctor clearly expected that I had been told of this conversation or would be told later. But it never happened.'

Science and Policewomen

Although the effectiveness of fingerprinting was well known it was not until 1902 that fingerprint evidence was accepted for the first time in an English court, with the conviction of a burglar called Henry Jackson.

Forensic firearm science was developed by a Dorset man, Ted Churchill, who came from near Bridport and served his apprenticeship with C. Jeffery, the Dorchester gunsmiths, before moving to London. In 1900 he became the advisor to the Metropolitan Police on gun-related murder cases. His nephew Robert later took over the business and set up his own test firing range and laboratory in the cellars of his shop behind the National Gallery. In 1927 he assisted Sir Wyndham Childs, then head of the CID to set up a permanent forensic firearms unit at New Scotland Yard.

In 1934 Dorset detectives were sent to New Scotland

Fingerprints are still an important part of crime detection. Aluminium powder is now used to highlight the prints as this photograph taken in 1985 shows.

In 1935 the force used cars for the first time to patrol the county.

Yard for an intensive course in the theory and practice of criminal investigation. Regional Forensic Science laboratories were also established. The one serving Dorset was at Bristol, from where experts gave a series of lectures, with officers later visiting the laboratory to receive practical instruction as to the kinds and quantities of material upon which scientific evidence could be given.

Of equal importance to the developments in forensics was the appointment of the first woman in the Dorset Constabulary, Helen Court, who transferred from Bristol City Police in 1937. Not only was she the first woman, she was probably the first university graduate of either sex to join the Dorset Force (she had an MA from Aberdeen University). Prior to her appointment, statements in indecency cases, or other cases regarded as too delicate for men to deal with, were taken from women and girls by local welfare workers or the Sisters of Mercy. Police wives living in or near the station were also used and paid 1s 6d an hour as 'Police Matrons' when women and girls were arrested. PWC Court was kept fully occupied until her transfer to Brighton in 1942, where she was promoted to sergeant.

Until 1947 in some forces, but later in Dorset, women could no longer continue serving if they married, and their careers therefore were often short-lived. During the war women auxiliary police officers were employed as shorthand typists, clerks or telephonists. Peggy Jeffers joined as a WAPC in 1941 and worked as a shorthand typist in the CID at Poole before becoming a regular policewoman in 1943, but she had to resign when she married Detective Constable Alfred Barrett in 1949. Joyce Pitman joined the Force in 1946 and left in 1949 to marry PC Leslie Barnes. She was later to become the first woman member of the Dorset Special Constabulary, serving until 1969.

Woman Police Constable Joan Tanswell, one of only eight women in the force at the time, seen here during the visit of HM The Queen to Dorchester in 1952.

FIVE

The Second World War

AT THE BEGINNING OF 1938, war with Germany threatening, a 'War Department' was formed for the purpose of training the Regular and Special Constabulary in Civil Defence and other war duties. The single storey divisional building at the Dorchester police station had an extra storey added and a new office building erected with a gas instruction room. Gas as a weapon was widely expected to be used, and the whole Force was well prepared and trained in dealing with it when war was declared on 3rd September.

As in 1914, there was an immediate recall to the Force of 73 police pensioners, known collectively as the First Police Reserve. Among the reservists was Leslie Fudge's father, who had originally joined in 1899 and retired in

The 1936 intake of recruits were so successful in the Annual Constabulary Sports meeting that a photograph was taken to record their achievements. The recruits, PCs Lewis. Lough, Russell, Coltart, Ash and Reed are shown with their trophies and prizes, including an armchair, bureau and canteens of cutlery.

1924. His return to uniform was even more remarkable as not only Leslie but three of his brothers were also in the Force, making a family of five all serving at the same time.

Another pensioner was PC Walter Billett who had had joined the Force in 1905 after serving in the army in China and South Africa and had retired in 1931. He rejoined at the age of 60 and cycled from his home in Broadstone to Poole Police Station to carry out his duties. In 1940 he fell off his bike in the blackout and tragically died shortly afterwards. His wife, although having to make do on a fifth of her husband's pension, her house lit by oil lamps and cooking in an oven heated by paraffin, still managed to take in four boy evacuees from Brixton.

A bombing campaign was widely expected, with the result that buildings were sandbagged and windows taped. A Special Branch was formed with officers in each division, trained to deal with Oswald Mosley's British Union of Fascists and other subversive elements. Uniformed officers made sure that the lighting regulations were complied with, that vehicles had their headlights blinkered and there were no chinks in the 'blackout'. The Chief Constable issued a directive that no German or Austrian male between the ages of 16 and 60 would be allowed to enter the county without his permission and any such aliens found in the county would be interned.

With the fall of France in 1940, small boats and fishing vessels began to sail into Poole Harbour, often laden to the gunwales with refugees clutching whatever they were able to carry. Owing to the risk of enemy agents among them, all arriving refugees were taken into custody and, with the assistance of military security officers, sent to Brownsea Island. In 1949 Dr Chesney, the medical officer of the Port of Poole reported that three spies were caught at Poole during the war – two men and a 'beautiful blonde' – two

BOBBIES ON THE BEAT / 45

of whom were executed. Poole Harbour also welcomed boatloads of British and French soldiers arriving from Dunkirk and Northern France, unshaven, battle-stained and exhausted.

Wartime Crime

Crime during the war continued and even increased. Nationally the number of murders went up from 288 in 1940 to 492 in 1945. Cases of rapes rose from 99 in 1937 to a peak of 416 in 1943. Looting offences went from nil in 1939 to 561 in 1944 but dropped to 93 in 1945. There was more opportunity with the country blacked out and a greater incentive with many products hard to come by.

A lot of the crime was minor; for example in March 1940 PC Taylor noticed a light in Woolworth's shop in Dorchester at 11.30pm. On investigating he found three soldiers escaping through the roof and after chasing them across the rooftops captured one of them. They all appeared in court the following month charged with breaking and entering and stealing a candle worth 1d and 7d in cash.

Criminals could also be young, two boys aged 15 and 16 were accused of discussing setting up a gang to terrorise the district where they lived in Weymouth. They were later charged with breaking into cars and shops and stealing what they could. The younger boy was put on probation for 12 months and the older one was sent to an approved school for the same length of time.

Pat O'Hara, a constable in Shaftesbury during the war, remembered it as lively and a more interesting place than in peacetime, with troops in the town, frequent air raid warnings, male and female military personnel to be billeted, severe traffic jams, and rising crime figures. He also had a military hospital on his patch at Guy's Marsh, a six mile journey by foot, bringing the extra work of accident and coroner's reports.

With the war continuing, the Germans dropped two delayed action parachute mines, specially constructed booby traps aimed at killing the anti-mine specialists at Portland. One drifted inland and was found by PC Fish at Doles Wood in Piddlehinton. He escorted Lieutenant Commander Anderson and Mr Leonard Walden, a civilian scientist, to the spot where it had landed, where with other men from the Bomb Disposal team they spent nearly a week dismantling it, making it safe and learning its secrets.

With the exception of Reservists with specialist qualifications, the Government decided it was best if policemen remained on home soil carrying out their usual duties. The Special Constabulary were playing an important role in policing and in many cases apart from the letters 'SC' on their collars were indistinguishable from their regular colleagues: up until the war 'Specials' had never been issued with uniforms, only with armbands and caps.

The Bombs start Falling

By the beginning of the war Jack Gray had moved from Wimborne, and later described the day the first bombs fell on Poole:

'In 1940 I was stationed at Market Street Police Station, on motor patrol. We had no radio but we did have a public address speaker. It was my duty to tour the town on 'Red Alert' broadcasting "there is an air raid warning in progress. You are advised to take cover". Up to then there had been no enemy activity and the public took little or no action apart from a friendly wave.

On the 21st August, a Wednesday afternoon, I was doing this duty and as I drove through the High Street my eldest brother, Arthur, who was on that beat, made me a rather unbrotherly gesture as I passed him. I arrived back at Market Street and parked. Tom Forsey, who was on guard outside the sand bags, shouted "lookout". I looked up to see a Junker 88 dropping a string of bombs directly overhead. Whilst I was taking this in, the bombs were down. One landed on 38 Market Street just below the station and the blast caught Tom and me and blew us along the pavement. I can still remember the rattle of Tom's Lee Enfield 303 as it clattered along with us. Apart from bruises and scratches we were uninjured but poor Mrs Pauline Fairbrother at No 38 was killed. She had been sheltering under her stairs, doubtless as a result of my warning.

The first bomb had landed on the National School's air raid shelter, thankfully not occupied, but Mr Landry who had been standing nearby, was also killed. The second had made a direct hit on the Fifty Shilling Tailors and the High Street was decorated with the dummies blown out of the shop still wearing their £2 10s suits. My brother Arthur was safe as he was by the library at the time. The third was the Market Street bomb and a fourth fell on Balson's shipyard causing some damage but no casualties. The next time I announced the warning I noticed a lot more attention was paid!'

Bombs or no bombs the magistrates still kept sitting and in the same year Albert Bulley from Owermoigne became the first person in the county to be summonsed for refusing to accept evacuees as lodgers. PC Barnes stated that Bulley, who had assumed a truculent manner, said he had a wife who was ill, a daughter and only two bedrooms. He was found guilty and fined £5. Wartime creates a necessary levelling of society, and appearing at Blandford Court at about the same time were two men not usually seen in the dock of a court. One was Viscount Cranborne, the Member of Parliament for South Dorset, the other the Lord Lieutenant, Lord Shaftesbury, both of whom were charged, along with 18 others, of buying butter at more than the stipulated price (maximum retail prices had been put on most commodities). Lord Cranborne's defence that he did not concern himself with the domestic arrangements for food did not save him from a £2 fine with £2 costs.

Someone else to be fined was John Goatley, a Special Constable at Yetminster, who was sent to prison for a month and fined £5 with 12s 6d costs for making a statement connected with the war 'likely to cause alarm or despondency'. He was alleged to have said that 'In a week Hitler will be here. The King and Queen will be gone to Canada. The Duke and Duchess of Windsor will be in London and will be dictators to the Germans. There will be no unemployed when Hitler gets here. There will be plenty of work, but the wages will be low. Ireland will be the next place they would be in. I will make you a bet we will be under German rule within a fortnight.' He pleaded not guilty, denied having made the statement and said it must have been imagined.

The bombing phase now started, and on the 30th September 1940 at 4.15 on a Sunday afternoon 300 bombs fell on Sherborne in three minutes. Eighteen people were killed, 32 injured and 766 of the town's 1,700 houses were damaged or destroyed. It is thought that the German

Cheap Street, Sherborne, the day after the 1940 raid in which 18 people were killed.

bombers had been on their way to the aeroplane works at Filton, Bristol, and having been intercepted by a squadron of Hurricanes, two of which were brought down, instead dropped their bombs on Sherborne. It could have been much worse. If the bombing had occurred a quarter of an hour earlier, Foster's Infants School would have been full of children and the carnage would have been terrible – it received a direct hit and had to be demolished. The abbey, school and castle escaped the bombing but all the services were damaged, the telephone exchange received a direct hit, and all the roads and sewers were blocked. Miss W. Steel, supervisor of the telephone exchange, was awarded the George Cross for keeping the one telephone in use and the town in contact with the rest of the country.

Although bombs were dropping on Dorset even more were falling elsewhere, and under a Regional Reinforcement Scheme in which aid was provided by police forces to other areas, a contingent of policemen from Dorset was sent to Portsmouth to assist with the post-raid operations, following the heavy attacks on the city.

In 1941, the Home Office permitted young police officers to volunteer for flying duties with the RAF, and Constables Bennett, Allum, Carter, Lock, Stapleforth, Reed and Smith, immediately responded. Neville Carter, aged only 22, became the Force's first casualty of the war after colliding with another aircraft in mid-air when flying a Hurricane. He was the son of Superintendent Carter of Poole Division and had been stationed at Wimborne and Weymouth, where he had received a commendation for arresting an armed soldier who was breaking into a house.

Of the seven, four were never to put on their uniforms as police officers again. Following Carter's collision, Robert Bennett flew into a mountain-top in Ireland, Leslie Lock was lost in a bombing raid over Germany, and Harold Stapleforth went out on patrol in his Coastal Command Sunderland over the Atlantic and was never seen again.

In 1942 the government decided all policemen under the age of 25 would be called up. Of the officers who served in the Forces only one, Constable Henry Cross from Piddlehinton, lost his life – whilst serving as a Lieutenant in the Royal Artillery. The Police War Reserve filled the gaps created in the ranks by the absence of these men. At the beginning, the Reserve comprised only volunteers from the Special Constabulary and a few local men, but later, older men from further afield were enlisted who were permitted to do their National Service as policemen.

The Americans Arrive

With the arrival of the first Americans in Dorset, and preparations for the invasion of occupied Europe, the south coast was made a restricted area. The Americans brought not only food and luxuries but in some cases trouble.

There is little evidence left – the newspapers at the time did not report anything detrimental to the war effort – but by 1944 one in five of the residents of Lyme Regis was an American serviceman, and trouble was inevitable. The first Americans to arrive in the town were a battalion of black servicemen. As far as the local girls were concerned they were both exotic and wealthy. A few months later the white American 16th Infantry Regiment came to the town and made themselves equally welcome.

In late May 1944 an attempt by a black soldier to buy a lighter in a shop restricted to white soldiers only turned into a full scale race riot in which a black soldier was fatally stabbed through the heart by a bayonet. News of the murder quickly spread and groups of opposing soldiers soon came into the town centre armed with clubs, rifles and even machine guns. Although the resident American Military Police could do little to diffuse the situation, two local policemen turned up and although unarmed (perhaps indeed because of it) were able to restore calm and persuade both groups to return to their respective camps. There is no record of anyone being charged for the murder, maybe because the 16th Infantry was part of the 1st Division which landed on Omaha Beach a week or so later, and of whom 1,638 men were either wounded or killed.

Shortly before D-Day the police on Portland took part in a census of all its occupants. Each person was checked and if no reason was given for his or her being there they were given 24 hours to leave. Road checks were set up near Ferrybridge and Dorset constables and military police guarded the Railway Station in Weymouth. To aid the county force, a contingent of Leeds policemen was sent to Dorchester, many of whom volunteered to serve on Portland (despite the expectation of heavy bombing which thankfully never occurred) – an island that must have seemed like another world after their gritty northern city.

The preparations for the invasion of France was clear to all and D-Day was expected at any time, Dorchester was filled with military transport parked in the avenues under the trees and Weymouth and Portland harbours were full. On the night of 5th/6th June there was a continuous drone of aircraft and in the morning the harbours were empty – the invasion had begun.

One witness to these dramatic events was PC George Woodsford, the beat constable in Spetisbury, who on the afternoon of June 5 made what he thought was a routine

The War Memorial at Headquarters after a tablet recording those men of the Force who gave their lives during the Second World War had been unveiled.

ABOVE The Swanage Section 1941/42. Among their number are War Reserve Constables Grant, Hancock, Smith and First Reserve Constable Welch.

BELOW The members of the Special Constabulary stationed at Wool during the war, photographed in 1945.

visit to take a statement at RAF Tarrant Rushton. Although able to enter the airfield he had to obtain a pass from the adjutant before being permitted to leave and was sworn to secrecy as to what he had seen. For amongst the aircraft and gliders lined up on its runway were the six Horsa gliders, towed by Halifaxes, that took off shortly before midnight for France. On board, under the command of Major John Howard, were the first soldiers to land in occupied France – the men whose task it was to secure the two bridges over the River Orne, one of them the famous Pegasus Bridge. Among those then serving in the Army was PC Roland Oliver, who had volunteered for the Special Services Brigade led by Lord Lovat, and who was in the unit that relieved Major Howard's men at the bridge.

Not all the weaponry was in the hands of the forces. In May 1944, Constable Fudge was chasing two boys who had absconded from a Borstal across the fields at West Stafford, when one of them, Frederick Jennings, turned and fired five shots from a revolver at the policeman. One bullet hit Constable Fudge, causing a flesh wound in his thigh. Nevertheless, Jennings was captured and, shortly afterwards, with the assistance of Special Constable Ricketts, the other absconder, Robert Blackshaw, was also arrested. Both were sentenced to three years' imprisonment, the jury commending Constable Fudge for his bravery, which was recognised later by the King's Police Medal for gallantry.

Helping to bring a little light relief to the county at an Easter dance in Weymouth in 1945 was the Dorset Constabulary Dance Band. The band had evolved from the Constabulary Concert Party formed in about 1930 by DCC Alfred Barrett, who as a band member played banjo and guitar. Other members were Supt Ernie Rossiter on alto sax, Supt Arthur Knight (tenor sax), Insp George Gray (piano), Sgt Bill Chase (trumpet), PC Harry Moore (bass) and PC Roy Russell (drums), supplemented by John Cutting, Jack Whitehorn (before the war a player in a London nightclub) and Ronald Linton (previously the organist of the ABC cinema in Plymouth), who were serving in the forces in the county. The band continued playing for Police Balls and other charity events throughout the county until it was finally disbanded in 1957.

The Dorset Constabulary Concert Party who performed during the 1940s.

Others who wanted to have a little bit of fun in Weymouth during the 1945 Easter weekend were nine girls aged 14 to 21, found sleeping in army ambulances in the Odean car park. They were charged with unlawfully being in vehicles in the service of His Majesty. The first three to appear in court were Joyce Springer from Tilburn, Isabella Finnigan from Edinburgh and Thelma Pugh from Brecon. Inspector Foster, prosecuting, said Springer, who was 18, had been in the area for some time and had become a bit of a nuisance. She and Finnigan had been expelled from a respectable hotel a few days earlier where they had been smuggled in by two officers. Pugh had absconded from a home in Hereford where she had been sent as being in need of care and protection. Springer and Finnigan were sentenced to 2 months imprisonment and Pugh, who was aged 14, was remanded in custody for a week.

Gwendoline Pearson and Barbara Fox, both from Bristol, had been found with two American sailors, saying that they had missed their train and had nowhere to stay. Pearson who was 17 was sent to prison for 7 days and Fox to a remand home for 7 days. Patricia Paddock and Joyce Wells from Bristol with Valerie Jones from Merthyr Tydfil were also found with American sailors in an ambulance. When Wells denied being with a sailor Inspector Foster said 'It looks like there was one spare girl and one spare sailor.' Wells was sentenced to 14 days imprisonment for trespassing, Jones who had left home eight weeks previously was sentenced to two months and Paddock for one month.

The final girl was Olive Shinn from Dorset who was 21. Inspector Foster described her 'As rather wayward. She has no known occupation and it looks as if her livelihood is a rather precarious one.' Asked if she would return to her parents she said 'They would not have me.' She was remanded in custody for 7 days.

It was not only sleeping in ambulances that could get a girl into trouble, not returning milk bottles was taken just as seriously. Jenny Woodsford of Dorchester was fined £3 and ordered to pay £1 7s 11d for retaining 269 milk bottles belonging to the T.T. Milk Depot for an unreasonable time contrary to the provision of the Milk (Use of Bottles) Order, 1943. The Executive Food Office found 333 bottles in her rear garden, several of them broken and the majority dirty, Mrs Woodsford said she had a son who had been invalidated out of the army who was at death's door and a 9 year old daughter and had not been able to return them herself.

The Chief Constable reported that in 1944 there had been 2,539 indictable offences, an increase of 155 over the previous year and 2,358 persons that proceedings had been brought against. Property to the value of £36,732 was stolen of which £21,243 was recovered. The Force also carried out 318 investigations into violent or sudden deaths.

Dorset had not been bombed anything like as badly as cities such as Plymouth or Portsmouth, but even so the amount of damage was quite considerable. As one of its duties, the Force was responsible for recording the number and places in the county where bombs had been dropped. A copy of the map on which they were all pinpointed can be seen in the Keep Museum in Dorchester, and it shows that 280 people were killed with 237 seriously injured and 358 slightly injured. There were 4,307 high explosive bombs dropped (396 unexploded) as well as 37,007 incendiary bombs. Of the aircraft that crashed, 54 were British (8 in the sea) and 90 German (31 in the sea).

SIX

Towards the Centenary

ALTHOUGH the traditional duty of the police to preserve law and order went on uninterrupted by war, the special circumstances of the war years delayed improvements to the day to day needs of officers and their families. Apart from a prototype rural station built in Puddletown just prior to the war, the only modern houses available when peace returned in 1945 were the quarters attached to the Poole and Bridport police stations. Otherwise the standard of housing was far from satisfactory: in 1947 there were still 63 police houses with no bathrooms.

PC Pat O'Hara moved from Poole to Cattistock to become the village policeman in 1946, later recalling his arrival at the police house in Kennel Lane with a young wife who had lived all her life in Poole. On a bitterly cold January morning he found a damp, badly decorated home, with no bathroom or airing cupboard. The toilet was an outside bucket lavatory that flooded in heavy rain and in

The Sherborne Division proudly displaying their sporting trophies won during the 1953 season.

Sergeant Jack Clist. He was the sergeant in charge at Cerne Abbas from 1945 to 1953.

which he had to wear a raincoat and rest his feet on a chopping block. The only bright thing was that PC Dick Shipton, from the adjoining Maiden Newton beat, had lit a fire and helped them move in.

By 1956, no less than 135 houses had been built with small offices attached or purchased since the war. But even then 50 more houses were needed to replace sub-standard houses, and a further 56 to provide accommodation for the married officers still without homes of their own.

Pat O'Hara, after serving in the busiest station in Dorset, decided he needed a challenge to save himself from, as he puts it, 'going round the twist'. He found this in the village football team, then in a sorry state. After having called a meeting in the Fox and Hounds he became the secretary of the newly formed committee. Fêtes, dances and baby shows brought in funds from which new kit was bought. Colonel Batten, the local Master of the Cattistock Fox Hounds, became president and added to the funds. All became worthwhile when success came to the team and they won the Edwards Charity Cup in Bridport.

The increase of crime begun during the war continued. Burglars began targeting ordinary houses, where small sums of money were kept in biscuit barrels and handbags. One such offender admitted that he had broken into more than 150 small houses before he was caught – and sentenced to 3 years' imprisonment.

Post war shortages and the continuation of rationing brought a return to smuggling. In April 1947 information was received that a landing craft laden with French wines and spirits was intending to sail into the upper reaches of Poole Harbour, where at Arne a lorry was waiting for the goods to be landed. It was a bold plan, and the four smugglers must have thought themselves safe as their heavily laden lorry slowly made its way along the lonely road inland across the heath from Arne. Suddenly, the driver was horrified to see the way ahead completely blocked and a swarm of excise men and policemen waiting their arrival. Although their leader had a revolver in his pocket he made no attempt to use it and the whole gang was arrested. Wareham magistrates sentenced two of the smugglers to 12 months imprisonment with fines amounting to nearly £20,000 and confiscation of the liquor.

Chantmarle, the Jacobean manor house near Cattistock that between 1951 and 1995 was the police traning centre for the south-west. In the 18th century a ghost in the house is alleged to have screamed, 'Search for Wat Perkins'. This stopped after two workmen found a headless skeleton and on mentioning it to Kit Whistle, a widow living near by, were offered a cow if they said nothing about it. This caused suspicion and she later confessed to murdering a pedlar 22 years previously and was hanged.

No. 7 Police District Training Centre, Chantmarle

As the Force modernized, it became obvious that training new recruits required a different approach. Up until the 1930s virtually all training had been by 'learning on the beat'. On joining, recruits spent six weeks at Headquarters learning drill under the drill sergeant and absorbing the contents of Captain Amyatt Brown's 'Black Book'. For those officers with an appetite for drill, there was a chance to join the Assize Squad, which the drill sergeant also trained, and whose principal function was to escort the judge at the beginning of each Assize in Dorchester from the Shire Hall to St Peter's Church.

With a backlog of recruitment caused by the retention of officers over the normal age of retirement there was an influx of ex-servicemen wishing to join. The lack of training facilities was remedied by establishing training centres within each region. The centre for the south-west region of England (covering the counties of Gloucestershire, Wiltshire, Somerset, Dorset, Devon and Cornwall) was opened in 1951 at Chantmarle, a beautiful Jacobean

The staff and members of the first intake to Chantmarle in 1951.

manor house built in 1612 by the lawyer Sir John Strode near Cattistock. The intensive syllabus of the course covered law and procedure, life-saving, first aid, civil defence and drill. Demonstrations and mock courts were staged in order to give practical experience of police duty. Short refresher courses were taken at intervals of one and two years, before the recruit finally completed his probation period.

When the first intake arrived at Chantmarle they were greeted by its commandant, Chief Superintendent Cook from Bristol, and his staff of Inspector Horton (Gloucester), Inspector Gould (Somerset) and Sgt Victor Davis from Dorset, the drill and unarmed combat instructor.

PC Ron Beale was part of the first intake and recalled that Farmer Burts' grazing field was used as the sports field, its humps and bumps causing many to hobble back to their quarters with sprained ankles. For life-saving and swimming there was the ancient moat around the house.

There was no resident band, so for their passing out parade Ron Beale loaned Sgt Davis his record of Kenneth Alford's march 'Sons of the Brave', which was played through loudspeakers and gradually adopted by the centre as an appropriate piece of music. The course lasted for 13 weeks, after which the intake returned to their own force for further instruction in local procedures and systems.

This was provided in Dorset by a Training Branch, set up after the war to provide refresher training for returning servicemen and to the regular and special constabulary, on subjects such as new legislation, civil defence and contagious diseases of animals.

A government white paper had recommended that sergeants and newly appointed inspectors should have advanced training in leadership skills. This was implemented by the opening of the Police College at Ryton-on-Dunsmore in Warwickshire in 1948. Up until then advanced training had been limited to short courses at the Metropolitan Police College for detectives, photographers, fingerprint experts and other specialists.

Traffic Patrols

In 1947 petrol rationing came to an end. With half a million new vehicles coming onto the roads each year the growth of car ownership created a new problem for the police. In 1948 the first traffic patrol motorcycles after the war were introduced. These were three Triumph 500cc 'Speed Twins' ridden by Constables Frank Slade, Alfred Conner and Denzil Highmore.

In 1951 PC Highmore and his bike made a guest appearance in the feature film 'Brandy for the Parson' then being filmed in Dorset and starring Kenneth Moore, Jean Lodge and Charles Hawtrey. His part was to attend a road traffic accident on the Old Sherborne Road. This was staged by having an Austin 7 colliding with the back of a Bere Regis bus from which a pole was attached. The pole was designed to pierce the radiator of the car, a can of water would then be tipped over the engine and an impressive cloud of steam would rise. After many dummy runs to get not only the camera angles correct but also the speeds and braking coordinated the stuntman prepared for the scene. He drove up to the back of the bus, but the endless dummy runs had caused his brakes to overheat and the impact was more realistic than everyone intended. After running repairs to both driver and car there appeared to be no permanent damage. The bike Denzil was riding appeared on television thirty years later in a programme called 'Talking Bikes'. These motorbikes had no

ABOVE The patrol cars of the early 1950s. The building behind is shown with the extra storey added in 1938 to house a police war department.

RIGHT Constable 811 Denzil Highmore riding his Triumph 500cc 'Speed Twin' at West Bay. There was no leather clothing in those days!

windshields nor did the rider wear a helmet or special clothing. As they had no radio the only way they could report in was using a public telephone kiosk.

This was soon to end. Transmitters on Eggardon Hill and Bulbarrow were erected in 1951, and with information and control rooms constructed at Headquarters, the 12 patrol vehicles were able to keep in constant communication with the control room. Mobile patrols were now able to call for assistance or to obtain information via a radio.

In the previous year, Mr Alfred Barrett, the Assistant Chief Constable died in service. He had joined the Force forty-two years earlier in 1908. After quickly moving up the ranks he was promoted to superintendent in 1920. Three years later he was appointed Deputy Chief

The Women's Voluntary Service 'food flying squad' feeding members of the Dorset Special Constabulary after the 1955 parade in Dorchester.

Constable, despite only fifteen years service and being the most junior of Dorset's eight superintendents. The position of Deputy Chief Constable was an appointment, not a rank, but in 1942 when the new rank of Assistant Chief Constable was created Mr Barrett became the first person in the Force to hold it. Henry Lovell succeeded him.

Dogs and Mr Plod

As early as 1914 the Chief Constable had said he had no objection to policemen having a dog on duty with him provided it was an Airedale and not dangerous. But dogs only became official companions when a gift of three Alsatian puppies was made to the Force in the early 1950s and volunteer handlers at Portland and Poole began training them for police work. In 1953 a dog section was formally established, with kennels at Dorchester and a small dog van, so beginning a partnership between handler and dog continuing today.

Another creation of the 1950s was that of Enid Blyton's Noddy. The author took her holidays in Swanage and Studland and after befriending and watching the local village policeman, PC Christopher Rone, plodding up the hill, she created PC Plod. PC Rone was an ex-guardsman and looked nothing like the character, but he inspired the approachable PC Plod and was quite happy and proud to be associated with this children's fictional character.

A Royal Warrant instituted by King George VI in 1951 introduced the Police Long Service and Good Conduct Award, and in the same year the Standing Joint Committee recommended that the Chief Constable be the first recipient in Dorset. He in turn recommended 72 members of the Force, the first being Sergeant R. Archer who had served since September 1925.

In 1955 Major Peel Yates, after 31 years the longest serving Chief Constable in the country, reached retirement age and in his honour a parade was held by the Special Constabulary in Dorchester. The ceremony also had the added purpose of marking the service the 'Specials' had

The parade to mark the retirement of Chief Constable Major Peel Yates in 1955 and to recognise the contribution the Special Constabulary had made to policing the county. They are lined up on the Dorchester Barracks Square.

rendered so diligently during and after the war. He was succeeded by Ronald Berry Greenwood OBE, a forty-four-year-old former wartime Lieutenant Colonel and later Assistant Chief Constable of Lincolnshire.

Although finding the Force well disciplined, completely loyal and anxious to give of their best Mr Greenwood set up a review of the Force organisation. Among the accepted recommendations were:

1. Motorcycles be provided for the large and hilly beats of Broadwindsor, Yetminster, Moreton, Fontmell Magna and Hazelbury Bryan.

2. Manning of Lyme Regis, Beaminster and Swanage sectional stations from early morning to late at night be reduced.

3. Private line telephone system be reorganized, thus saving the service of a constable on night telephone duty in Sherborne.

4. The fleet of 12 wireless cars be used for 12 hours a day instead of 8 hours

5. Practically all constables employed on clerical, cleaning and other admin duties be replaced by civilians.

The strength of the Force was increased from 389 to 452, including 24 cadets, partly to offset the reduction in the working week to 44 hours. As an aid to recruitment the height standard was reduced by an inch to 5ft 9ins. The Special Constabulary had a strength of 800 men and 18 women and there were 40 men in the First Police Reserve.

Three 'Excelsior Talisman' rural patrol motorcycles with their riders at Dorchester.

Chief Constable Lt Col Ronald Berry Greenwood OBE, KPM.

Altogether 47 civilians were employed including part-time cleaners. The traffic fleet of 46 vehicles consisted of 12 radio cars, 14 section or CID cars, a large van, a dog van, four utility vehicles and 14 motorcycles.

Explosions and Flooding

The summer of 1955 had not been uneventful for the Force in other respects. The detritus of war was still causing heartbreak. On Friday 13th May schoolboys aged 12 to 13 from Forres School in Swanage were on their usual afternoon walk along the beach when five of the boys found a rusty object on the beach. It was an unexploded mine. On trying to force it open, it exploded, killing all of them: one boy was thought to have been blown into the sea and although his shoes were washed ashore, his body was never found.

On the morning of the 16th June in Portland Harbour, the submarine HMS *Sidon* with a crew of 47, had loaded two experimental practice torpedoes and had just cast off from her sister ship HMS *Maidstone* when one of the torpedoes exploded. Twelve men died in the forward compartments, seven were injured and the rest of the crew was affected by gas and smoke. The captain ordered the escape hatches to be opened and the crew escaped, leaving behind the dead. When the boat sank, she took with her another victim, the medical officer from HMS *Maidstone*. He had gone aboard and assisted several survivors out of the submarine but unnoticed had collapsed and died of asphyxiation.

During the afternoon and night of July 18th, extremely heavy and prolonged rain fell in the Weymouth area causing extensive flooding. Altogether 11 inches fell, a record that still stands in the *Guinness Book of Records* as the greatest amount of rain to fall in a 24 hour period in the United Kingdom. The most seriously affected area was in and around Upwey, where the shallow River Wey rose 5 feet in half-an-hour, quickly becoming a raging torrent and breaking its banks, forcing 600 people from their homes. The aptly named Watery Lane was inundated to a depth of 12 feet, and bungalows were submerged almost to roof level. Buckland Ripers, Friar Waddon and Coryates to the

west of Weymouth, and the holiday camps at Osmington and Bowleaze east of the town were also badly affected. In Weymouth itself the Park district became flooded and water entered the basements of houses on the Esplanade.

The Local Authorities, Civil Defence and the Women's Voluntary Service, together with the Police, quickly put emergency measures in hand. The Royal Marines Amphibious School at Hamworthy sent special craft and crews with which the stranded were rescued; the Army sent vehicles and men from Dorchester and Bovington Camp and supplied over 600 blankets for the homeless; and sailors from Portland assisted with underwater equipment. Bridport, West Bay, and Burton Bradstock were also

Among those delivering supplies and ensuring the safety of the inhabitants of Upwey is Constable Ron Wye who is rowing the boat. He may look happy but previously to this photograph being taken he had approached a house not knowing there were steps leading down and had all but disappeared except for his helmet.

seriously flooded, and many holiday campers had to be evacuated to rest centres from their tents and caravans. Fortunately, no lives were lost during the actual flooding, but the next evening a small boy fell into the flood water at Upwey, and, despite heroic attempts to save him, was swept away and drowned.

LEFT The Police Dog Section 1956. Although the dog's names are recorded their handlers are not. The dogs are Konig, Bess, Dana, Andi and Susan.

BELOW A police pillar in Poole in the 1960s.

Violent Incidents

At the start of 1956 Constable Stanley Cornick was awarded the British Empire Medal in the New Year Honours List for his bravery during a firearms incident at Fontmell Magna. Tamplin, a youth of 17, was friendly with a married couple and gradually became infatuated with the wife. Driven by jealousy, and armed with a .22 rifle, he waited for her husband to return from work, causing serious injuries. Tamplin made off, armed with the rifle, then stole a car, eventually overturning and abandoning it. A search by regular, special officers and dogs eventually tracked him down to a copse near Fontmell Magna. On being confronted by Constable Cornick and his dog Bess he took aim and fired, luckily missing both PC Cornick and his dog. He was overpowered and arrested. Appearing at the Dorset Assize in May, Tamplin was sentenced to 3 years imprisonment on a charge of attempted murder.

Another violent incident, this time domestic, involved Thomas Scott, aged 70, who attacked his wife with a billhook at their home in Verwood. Although seriously injured, she escaped to the next-door house of her son-in-law Frederick Barrow. A violent struggle ensued between Scott and Barrow, Scott resisted all efforts to be restrained and a rope was found and placed around his neck. He continued to fight and in an attempt to stop him the rope was pulled tighter until Scott ceased to struggle. When a doctor and the police were called they found Scott dead of strangulation. The son-in-law was charged with manslaughter at which he pleaded not guilty. The magistrates decided that but for his intervention other deaths might have resulted, his action was considered justifiable and he was discharged.

In 1956 the number of pillars in Poole was increased by 9 to 41. A police pillar had a warning light on top which could be turned on from the control panel in the Central Police Station. Ray Crickmore remembers some sites of the original pillars as No 1 being at the bottom of the High Street outside what was then the Seaman's Mission. Pillars 2 and 3 were along the Blandford Road in Hamworthy, No 4 was in the High Street near the old gas showrooms and Pillar 5 outside the Blandford Arms opposite the George Hotel. The pillars alerted the nearest patrolling officer, who by using the telephone could then be diverted to incidents or road accidents.

Ray's recollections of the early 1950s were not that different to what towns are like today. On Saturday nights the Quay beat in Poole was doubled up from 10pm to 1am. Coach loads of young soldiers from Bovington and Lulworth Camp descended on the town with the Labour Club Centenary Hall Dance being the major attraction. The soldiers caused little trouble unless they missed their last bus and then there were arrests for attempted and unauthorised taking of vehicles. There was, though, a local gang of troublemakers. One summer's night outside the Jolly Sailor Ray, with PC Bill Gurd, a big and sturdy man, broke up a fight between two groups. Bill was laying down the law when one of the troublemakers splashed a pint of beer over him. He reached behind and grabbed the first body he felt. It was the culprit, who was gripped firmly, put into a nearby taxi with Bill on top of him and driven off to Market Street.

The Force also had other matters to deal with. To keep up the belief that rural police forces only concern themselves with sheep the officers of the Force attended 171 dippings and observed the dipping of 22,344 sheep, half of the total of 44,301 dipped in the county.

Force trumpeters Habgood and Bishop playing at an Assize in Dorchester.

A rather more serious affair was the civil defence exercise held in the Chapelhay district of Weymouth in 1956. The Chapelhay area had suffered from bomb damage during the war and had yet to be redeveloped. The Cold War and fear of a nuclear attack pervaded much of the 1950s. In 1956 the county civil defence warden section had a strength of 1,076 members and air raid sirens were regularly tested right up until 1962.

The Athletics Club held its 50th Annual Sports Meeting at Dorchester to which 5,000 people attended. Officers of the Force also organised, in their own time, Boys Clubs at Blandford, Ferndown and Poole. Activities included outdoor and indoor games, handicrafts and canoeing. The Poole club had a membership of 60 boys and supplied half the Dorset Association of Boys Clubs' football team. They were a successful team, reaching the national final where the London ABC narrowly beat them. Members of the Force remained involved with youth organizations. In 1967, the last year figures were collated, twelve officers

The annual Dorset Constabulary Athletics Club sports meetings at Dorchester were still drawing in crowds of 5,000 in the early 1950s.

were involved in youth clubs, another eight held administrative posts in the Boy Scout movement, four in the Sea Cadet Corps and three held officer rank in the Army Cadet Corps.

The Centenary Celebrations

The highlight of 1956 was the celebration of the 100th anniversary of the Force, which was marked by a parade held in September in Dorchester. The contingents, made up of regular officers, members of the Special Constabulary, police cadets, recruits in training from Chantmarle, police pensioners, motor patrol vehicles and the dog section, were led by the band of the Queen's Bays (2nd Dragoon Guards).

After marching from Queen's Avenue to the Depot Barracks of the Dorset Regiment they were inspected by the Lord Lieutenant, Lord Digby, after which the Bishop of Sherborne conducted a service. Later the Chairman of the Standing Joint Committee opened an exhibition of the history of the Force at County Hall, which attracted 8,000 visitors in the week it was open. In that way the first one hundred years of the Dorset Constabulary was marked, so ending a centenary of service.

SEVEN

A Changing Society

THE NEXT fifty years were to see many changes, not only technically but also within society and the police. The fifties saw the birth of rock and roll, and an increasingly affluent society, many of whom were young.

In keeping with this less formal atmosphere uniforms were given a new look when from April 1957 open neck jackets and helmets replaced closed neck jackets and caps.

There was still crime, as is illustrated by a list of all the offences committed in Dorset on a single day sometime in 1957.

Unlawful wounding at Poole
Theft of a wrist watch at Parkstone
Indecent assault on a boy of 7 at Parkstone
Theft of a knitted pullover at Sandbanks
House breaking with intent at Wool
Theft of growing crops at Stratton
Theft of a fountain pen at Lulworth
Housebreaking at West Moors
Theft of a newspaper at Poole
Theft of 1½ bottles of milk at Weymouth
Theft of sewage pipes at Lodmoor.

Some events other than crime could catch the Force off-guard, such as a celebrity wedding in Poole in the summer of 1958. PC John Matthews was patrolling the Longfleet beat when someone commented to him he was in for a busy day and showed him a piece in a Sunday newspaper announcing the marriage of the England and Wolves footballer Billy Wright to Joy Beverley, of the then popular girl group 'The Beverley Sisters', taking place in Poole that same day. He immediately informed the duty Inspector.

PC Den Damen was cycling into Market Street police station when Sergeant John Foster came out and told him to follow him to the Registry Office in Parkstone Street. While cycling there the sergeant commented 'There's

Although Dorset Constabulary had a dog section other forces did not. These two Dorset dogs and their handlers were assisting the Bristol City force during a murder enquiry.

elephants, camels, the lot going to be there.' At the time there was a circus on the 'Lady's Walking Field'.

Den Damen recalls:

'When we arrived at the Registry Office there was a crowd of about 200 people outside but this quickly grew to about one thousand. Then from the Park Gates direction came a purple Vauxhall Cresta car driven by the Beverley Sister's father with their mother in the front and the three sisters in the back seat, followed by a blue Hillman driven by Billy Wright. The crowd went mad and surrounded the two cars. The bridegroom asked me to park the two cars giving me the ignition keys. By this time the duty inspector had arrived on the scene and told me to park them in Elizabeth Road. Traffic had been brought to a standstill by then and I only just managed to get through the crowd.

When the family came out of the Registry Office, such was the

The Assize Squad and the judge proceeding up High West Street, Dorchester in 1955.

crowd, Teddy Beverley lost one of her shoes and asked me to find it, and although I looked it was nowhere to be seen – someone had walked off with it. Monday's newspaper commented that while the sergeant was controlling the crowd all by himself the constable just stood in the crowd enjoying himself.'

Crime remained at the top of the agenda, the Chief Constable in his annual report at the end of 1958 wrote: 'The continued increase in crime presents one of the most serious social problems of the day. In Dorset, crime has risen again by 10%. Although the present wave of lawlessness is by no means confined to adolescents, national statistics show they are responsible for nearly one third of all detected offences: those in the age group 17 to 21 who have been convicted of crime has more than doubled within the past 20 years.

'There are many theories as to the causes of the general deterioration in moral standards but it would seem to be in that age group that the circumstances of their birth and upbringing may well have a great deal to do with it.

'Whatever the causes of crime may be, the task of maintaining control of the situation lies squarely on the shoulders of the police. Bearing in mind that in 1938, the total number of indictable crimes in Dorset was only 1,424, compared with 4,210 in 1958, almost three times as

many, it is apparent that the task is not an easy one and calls for constantly increased efficiency, coupled with an endless search for more effective counter measures.'

Unwelcome Visitors

If mundane crime was not enough to deal with the Force was not spared having to deal with the IRA. In the early hours of Sunday February 16 1958 an IRA raiding party of seven men dressed in military clothing attacked Blandford Camp. Five armed men entered the armoury guardroom and bound and gagged the corporal and four soldiers at gunpoint. The other two ambushed the patrolling guard of two young national servicemen and attempted to grab their rifles. One stoutly resisted and was shot in the stomach, though not seriously injured. The other guard was eventually overpowered after a struggle and both were taken to the guardroom and tied up.

A civilian telephone operator who heard the shots informed the sergeant in the main guardroom. When he went to investigate he was overpowered along with two other soldiers who were returning to their quarters, and they were also taken to the guardroom and tied up. Something though panicked the raiding party, and they drove away.

Within a few minutes the guard had untied themselves and sounded the alarm. The police were notified at 2am and officers were immediately sent to the camp. In the lane leading to the camp they found an abandoned car, inside which was a fully loaded magazine for a Thompson sub-machine gun and some chisels and screwdrivers. The car belonged to a car hire firm in London. Nothing else was found despite a search by police dogs.

On the following Monday enquiries revealed that an Irishman had been staying at a house in Charlton Marshall in which was found a quantity of military clothing, as well as a revolver, and ammunition.

His description was circulated and a car belonging to him was found at Southampton on Tuesday. The police in Bournemouth discovered that the same man had hired a 'mobile home' at Wallisdown earlier in the month, in which more military uniforms and a variety of firearms

and ammunition were found. It transpired the gang had fled to Eire and as a result no arrests were made.

Brian Melvin, as a constable in Poole, also had a small part to play in this incident. He was alerted by Pillar No. 6's flashing light at 3.30am, and on picking up the telephone was informed by the duty sergeant of the raid and instructed to return to the Central Station. There he was ordered to collect a bicycle and red lamp and set up a roadblock at Fleetsbridge. On enquiring who would accompany him, he was told he was on his own. The one patrol car had gone to Blandford and he was the only beat man available. As he remarked, perhaps it was as well that the IRA decided not to tangle with the might of Poole Division that night.

Fighting crime was made easier by the opening of the Regional Criminal Record Office for No. 7 Police District and a new photographic laboratory at Headquarters. Colour transparencies were produced in courts in the county for the first time in criminal proceedings and communications were speeded up when a teleprinter was installed.

Crime comes in all shapes and sizes. The Metropolitan Police informed the Force that two wanted men might be

ABOVE Constable John Calder proudly stands beside his new Ford Zephyr. Note the loudspeaker and bell on the front.

BELOW Making a Conference Point at Holnest Cross on the A37 near Evershot.

Dorset Constabulary helmet plate in use from 1957 to 1967.

coming to Dorset in order for one of them to visit his parents. Later enquiries revealed that one man was masquerading as a woman and wearing a nylon fur coat. Motor patrols were instructed to keep a look out for possible sightings. When a police patrol came across two people hitchhiking, possibly fitting the description, they were given a lift. The 'wife' was tall, slim and elegantly dressed in a black dress, nylon fur coat and white high-heeled shoes. Her face was well made up and her appearance was made more convincing by an excellently styled head of black hair. Beneath the effeminate voice, however, the unmistakably deeper tones of a man could be detected. Upon being challenged, the masquerader removed the wig and admitted his identity. He had changed his clothes on the London to Bath train in an attempt to avoid being recognised, but the disguise didn't fool the Constabulary and both men were sentenced to long prison sentences.

The Cold War

Disguise of a different kind was involved in 1960 when information was passed to Weymouth Detective Constable Leonard Burt by a naval security officer that Harry Houghton, a clerk, was spending far more than he was earning. This intelligence was to eventually lead to the Portland Spy Case and to the arrest and conviction of a Russian spy master. Harry Houghton and his girlfriend, Ethel Gee, were clerks at the Admiralty Underwater Weapons Establishment on Portland and were later found guilty of passing information to Helen and Peter Kroger.

The Krogers were living in Ruislip and claiming to be from Canada, but were really Morris and Lona Cohen from the USA, recruited in 1938 by the Russians. They in turn reported to Gordon Lonsdale (KGB Director, Georgi Lonoff) who had also been born in the USA and by posing as a US Naval Commander had persuaded Houghton and Gee to steal secret material for which they would be paid.

They were paid well. When newly promoted Sgt Burt searched Harry Houghton's Weymouth house he found £500 in premium bonds, another £650 in a plastic bag hidden in a paint tin in the garden shed as well as navigational charts of Portland Harbour and a plan under the false bottom of a matchbox. In Ethel Gee's Portland house he found a list of 18 secret file reference numbers and in three handbags money and shares to the value of £4,745. Ethel Gee was earning £10 a week at the time. They were both sentenced to 15 years imprisonment. Although Lonsdale was sentenced to 20 years imprisonment, he was later exchanged for Greville Wynne, a British businessman in 1964. Helen and Peter Kroger were released in 1969 in exchange for Gerald Brooke after serving eight of their 20 year sentence.

In August the same year disaster struck Lyme Regis when a furniture van carrying 35 London Boy Scouts and their camping equipment went out of control through brake failure. The van went through a shop window, knocked down numerous pedestrians and a lamp post, causing severe damage to several stationary and moving vehicles. The scene was reported to have resembled a battlefield. Two people were killed, one of them a toddler, 18 others were injured and 14 vehicles were damaged.

Status Quo

A Royal Commission was set up in 1960 to consider among other things whether local forces should remain or whether there should be a national police force. The majority of the commission decided to support the status quo. The Home Secretary, Rab Butler, agreed and said 'I am quite convinced that it would be quite wrong for one man or one government to be in charge directly of the whole police of this country. Our Constitution is based on checks and balances. This has kept our liberty throughout generations.'

The same Royal Commission also recommended that from September 1960 a constable's pay should start at £600 per annum, rising to £970 after 22 years service with the addition of free housing, uniforms and allowances.

Bishop's Caundle Parish Council tried to make their own contribution to a constable's pay when they collected 2s 6d from each of 300 parishioners for a retirement gift to PC Maurice Legg to, as parish councillor Phillips said

ABOVE In the late 1950s patrol cars appeared with a blue light on the roof for the first time.

BELOW The information room at Dorchester in the 1960s.

Chief Constable Arthur Hambleton CBE, MC, QPM, DL.

The Constabulary Headquarters entrance arch in 1962.

'show our appreciation of an exceptional and ideal village constable'. Unfortunately they had to get permission from the Standing Joint Committee, which was refused, the Chief Constable telling them that if they gave it without permission PC Legg's pension would be forfeit.

A sign of things to come was the purchase of a radar speed meter, or to give it its full title a 'Portable Electronic Traffic Analyser'. Following its introduction signs were erected at the county boundaries on all major roads announcing 'Dorset Police check speed by radar'. In September of the following year a modernised control room at Dorchester started operating. Two-way radio communications were fitted into all traffic cars and a new wireless station and aerial erected on Bulbarrow Hill. The 999 emergency telephone call system had just been introduced into the county and was reported to be working satisfactorily.

Lt Colonel R. B. Greenwood left the Force in November 1961 to become Chief Constable of Devonshire. He was replaced by Mr Arthur Hambleton MC, whose police career began in 1937 when he joined the West Riding Constabulary. In 1942 he joined the Royal Marines where he was awarded the Military Cross for Gallantry and Distinguished Service in North West Europe, later becoming an Acting Major. He returned to the West Riding Constabulary in 1946 and was promoted sergeant in the same year. Quickly rising through the ranks, he spent a year as Director of Studies at the Police College before being appointed Assistant Chief Constable of the Cardiff City Force in 1955.

The people of Dorset took a keen interest in their local police, as shown by the 3,000 people who visited Dorchester Police Station during an 'open week' in July 1962. The following year road safety lectures were attended by 12,460 children in 33 schools, 1,435 children entered the National Cycling Proficiency Scheme and 2,731 people attended lectures and films showing advanced driving techniques. One exception was the crowds attending the Annual Constabulary Sports; they had been decreasing over the years and in 1963 the 57th meeting became the last to be held.

An increase in strength of 97 over four years, a large increase considering the total number of the Force was only 471, was initiated after a working week of 42 hours was introduced. The beats were reduced from 47 to 22 and because they covered a larger area 21 extra motorcycles were acquired. Altogether the Force deployed 12 patrol cars, 17 other cars, 44 beat motor cycles and 14 vans.

Patrolling officers were issued with a credit card system to use in public telephone kiosks, which had gradually become common. This was to seal the end for police pillars in Poole, and in time they were dismantled. Appearing for the first time in 1965 were 'walkie talkies', when the first four sets were obtained.

Teddy Roe is Banned

Unsocial behaviour made an appearance in Sherborne during the Pack Fair. Originally the week long fair opened at midnight on a Sunday in October when a noisy procession called Teddy Roe's Band paraded through the town making 'rough music'. This was followed by the cattle, sheep and horse sale on Monday. Teddy Roe is thought to have been the foreman of the workmen who repaired the Abbey after it was nearly destroyed by a fire. As long ago as in the reign of Henry VIII there were complaints that 'labourers and artificers used their riotous expenses and unlawful games to the great trouble and inquieting of the inhabitants next thereto adjoining.'

The *Dorset Evening Echo* reported in 1962 that 'instead of waiting for the stroke of midnight a group of youths bent on trouble jumped the gun and started off from Bristol Road three minutes early. Hundreds of revellers, many armed with so-called musical instruments – broken down bugles, rattles, oil drums etc. followed. Before long the procession struggled over a mile. The police, especially reinforced from other parts of the county, managed to contain the procession to the route. The head of the column had covered the town and reached the town centre in 40 minutes, normally it takes an hour or more. While many couples twisted and rocked to recorded music, in the town centre reports of damage started coming in. More than 20 house windows were smashed, 17 in Long Street alone.' Despite a large police presence in 1963 there was still vandalism, whilst in October 1964 The *Dorset Evening Echo* reported: 'More than 100 extra police moved into Sherborne last night – to back up the order by

The cliff rescue squad in action in the 1980s.

the Chief Constable banning the midnight march of the tin-can band. Some policemen had walkie-talkie radios. Police dogs waited with handlers and Teddy Roe didn't play a note. The only incident came when two young men unfurled a large red and white banner painted 'Ted must not die – Council must ban martial law.' Slumbering Sherborne was undisturbed. The band remained banned until the 1970s.

A cliff rescue squad was formed the same year with the participants being trained by the Royal Marines. The squad quickly made an impact. The following year Constable Kenneth Pearce was awarded the BEM for gallantry when assisting Coastguard Officer Plant in rescuing a man from the cliffs at Worbarrow and the year

Police Mobile Columns were intended to be ready to police a 'Z Zone', an area in which a nuclear bomb had been dropped.

after that he was awarded a Certificate of Merit by the RSPCA for attempting to rescue cows from cliffs at White Nothe.

In November 1966 a 28 year old Borstal officer died in a brutal assault at the Portland Borstal. The search for the suspects, two Borstal boys who had escaped, involved over 400 people including police and prison officers. A contingent of over 100 police officers who had been training in Wiltshire as part of the Police Mobile Column also helped out. After two days searching the escaped boys were found and arrested, and one was later charged with the murder.

Police Mobile Columns were formed in 1965 to police areas devastated in a nuclear attack. These were the predecessors of Police Support Units, and the columns were made up of officers from the different forces within each region. The column had a strength of about 100 officers under the command of a superintendent, and was divided into sections of a sergeant and ten constables. The columns used Home Office vehicles and were self-contained, providing their own catering and communications.

The number of civilian vehicles licensed in the county had risen to 11,904 by 1966. The Force annual report commented that 'in the saturation periods of the summer months the level of congestion reached a stage of "traffic thrombosis" especially in coastal areas . . . drastic forms of

The Women's Life Saving Team in 1964. Showing from the top Constables Collier, Mills, Roper, Mack, Needham and Sergeant Gracie.

control are becoming inevitable to ensure uninterrupted movement.' It went on to record a dramatic reduction in the number of fatal accidents in the county from 68 in the previous year to 41, concluding that the innovation of a 70mph speed limit may have had a bearing on this.

Other 'drastic action' was also taken when Poole became the lucky town to have the first traffic wardens in the county.

The following year the Dorset Constabulary and the Bournemouth Police amalgamated, becoming the Dorset and Bournemouth Constabulary.

A traffic warden controlling traffic in Branksome, Poole.

EIGHT

Bournemouth enters Dorset

BETWEEN 1948 AND 1967 the Borough of Bournemouth had been policed by a Borough Force, and before that by Hampshire Constabulary.

When the Hampshire Constabulary was formed in 1839, Bournemouth was described as a small 'watering place', part of the parish of Holdenhurst. Although from 1856 to 1858 Constable Smith was the only policeman in what is now Bournemouth, the community quickly increased in size. By 1869 a police station had been built in Oxford Road (now Madeira Road) manned by a sergeant and two constables.

Even though small, reinforcements were sometimes required from other parts of Hampshire to police the town for the November 5th celebrations. They travelled in plain clothes, taking their uniforms with them in a carpet bag so as to disguise their identity. When they finally reached Bournemouth they were well looked after. To recover from the journey each officer was given ¾lb of cold meat, ½lb bread and 2 pints of beer (only one pint to be drunk before going on duty).

The town grew so rapidly that by 1882 the Bournemouth Commissioners were considering petitioning Queen Victoria for the grant of a charter to constitute the town as a Municipal Borough. Two years later an inspector was put in charge at Oxford Road and other stations opened at Pokesdown, Springbourne, Moordown and Westbourne. For the 1890 opening of the Poole Road Hospital by the Prince and Princess of Wales a force consisting of Hampshire's Chief Constable, 6 superintendents, 3 inspectors, 19 sergeants and 116 constables was considered necessary.

The town reached divisional status in 1892 when the strength had risen to 44 men with Superintendent Knapton being appointed to lead them. They took their duties

Constable David Barnes served at Holdenhurst from March to June 1855. He was pensioned off in 1877.

The first Bournemouth police station in 1875. Sergeant Catchlove was the officer in charge with a strength of three constables.

Boscombe police setting off for an outing in August 1908.

seriously. A Mr Butterworth was fined £1 or ten days in prison for refusing to take his dog off the pier, as was Luke Holden for bathing on a 'part of the beach not set aside for the purpose'.

Superintendent Samuel Foster took over in 1895 and had the advantage of having a telephone installed in the police stations at Bournemouth and Boscombe, (built in 1893 in Gloucester Road). Superintendent Foster and Sergeant Thomas were commended and awarded £5 and £2 respectively by the Police Authority for arresting burglars wanted by Dorset Constabulary. The burglars must have been a dangerous pair, the superintendent had used a revolver to arrest them.

At the turn of the century the *Bournemouth Directory* complained that the £5,000 it was costing the borough for policing was far more than other similar towns.

In 1904 Samuel Foster died while attending a funeral and Walter Hack took over. He and his men could sometimes rely on the co-operation of the public. Eighteen year old Florence Edwards saw a crowd watching PC Sainsbury being attacked by a man in Wimborne Road. With another bystander and despite the threats of a crowd, she forced her way to the side of the policeman, fearlessly blowing his whistle until other constables arrived and arrested Sainsbury's attacker. For her courage she was presented with a gold medallion inscribed 'For Bravery'

and the police gave her a gold bangle inscribed, 'Presented to Florence Edwards by Bournemouth Police for assistance rendered on 21 December 1907'.

Shadrack Garrett succeeded Superintendent Hack in 1919 and was later awarded the MBE. The *Bournemouth Guardian* described him as 'a man of character, he has a fine figure doing credit and giving dignity to his position, is remarkably popular with his men although rigid in discipline, is capable and efficient, has a very courteous and happy manner and conceals a kindly heart and a real desire to help the erring ones under his official aspect.' He retired in 1927 and was succeeded by William Deacon.

In 1934 Constable Hugh Pirnie was awarded the King's Police Medal for gallantry for arresting a thief who was disturbed in a jeweller's shop in Westover Road. He escaped into the Pleasure Gardens and was pursued by members of the public and police. PC Pirnie caught up with him near the Bourne Stream where the thief turned and pointed a loaded automatic pistol at him shouting 'Up or I fire.' Ignoring the threat, PC Pirnie tackled the man

and after a violent struggle overpowered and arrested him.

Although a request from the Borough Council for a policewoman to be appointed was originally turned down, it was granted its wish during the Second World War when six auxiliary policewomen were recruited.

They soon proved their worth, for Bournemouth's coastal position placed it firmly in the front line during the Second World War. The worst air raid took place in May 1943, twelve German planes dropped four tons of high explosive on the town, the Metropole Hotel in the Lansdowne and the Central Hotel in Richmond Hill were both hit and Beales Department store was burnt out. Altogether 77 people were killed, including American, Australian and Canadian troops billeted in the Metropole, although the number of casualties would have been much higher had not the bombing occurred during Sunday lunchtime when the streets were fairly quiet.

Superintendent Osman, who had been appointed in 1938, was promoted to chief superintendent in recognition of Bournemouth being the largest County Borough in

ABOVE Bournemouth bobbies cool off before entering the 1939 uniform race in the Bournemouth Regatta.

BELOW His Majesty's Inspector of Constabulary inspecting Bournemouth police at Boscombe in about 1947.

England to be policed by a County Constabulary. He was later posted to Winchester and Sydney Bennett took over.

It was Sydney Bennett who was appointed the first Chief Constable of the Bournemouth Borough Police force when, after a deputation to the Home Secretary, a decision was made to establish an independent force. It came into being on the 1st April 1948 with an establishment of 191 men and 4 women. Among the appointments was Hugh Pirnie who was now an inspector and put in charge of Winton Section.

In May, 1954, Chief Constable Bennett and Detective Superintendent Spooner of Scotland Yard led the investigation into the murder of Miss Amy Lloyd who, aged 74, was known as the mother of St Andrew's Cub Scout Pack. She was found inside the front door by her companion Miss Gifford, with 29 knife wounds. The Chief Constable told reporters that the crime appeared to be completely motiveless and whoever committed it 'must have been mental.'

After a youth of 16 or 17 was seen cycling near the scene, investigations centred on the Scout movement, with hundreds of scouts over the age of 15 being interviewed. Among those interviewed was a 16-year-old boy who had appeared in the Bournemouth *Daily Echo* as having gained the Queen's Scout Award. Later it transpired that he had forged various certificates connected to the award, to which he was not entitled. While he was at the police station being questioned his room was searched and a sheaf knife and bloodstained scout uniform were found. These had been washed and it was not possible to match the blood with that of Miss Lloyds. He was later charged with the murder and sentenced to be detained during Her Majesty's pleasure. He was released a few years later.

The Great Train Robbery of a night mail train in August 1963 shocked the nation. An audacious 15 strong gang led by Bruce Reynolds had stolen £2.5 million. In Bournemouth, Mrs Clarke, the widow of a policeman, had reported two 'dodgy characters' who had paid to rent her garage with money taken from a large wad of ten shilling notes. DC Peter Stuchbury at Bournemouth Police Station took the call but was too busy dealing with a stolen bicycle, instead DC Charlie Case and Sergeant Stan Davies

went to check it out. While they were at the address in Tweedale Road, two men drove up in a grey Austin 30 van. After the policemen had asked them if they could look inside it, and been refused, a struggle took place, one of the men hanging onto the car roof for dear life and shouting out that they were being mugged, convincingly enough for neighbours to go out to help them. It was not until uniformed officers turned up that they realised the plain clothes detectives were policemen. After examining the van, £78,892 in cash was found. The men were arrested and taken to the police station where they were identified as Roger Cordrey and Bill Boal. Cordrey was a thief and as an ex-railway worker had been employed by the 'Great Train Robbery' gang to fix the railway signal. More money was found in another vehicle, making a total of £141,000. At Aylesbury, where they were the first of those connected to the robbery to appear in court, they were sentenced to 14 years imprisonment. Boal, who was a friend of Cordrey was employed by him to help hide the loot. The length of his sentence seemed rather harsh considering he was not in the original gang and the only one to plead guilty.

In 1958 Sydney Bennett had retired and Donald Lockett, formerly the Chief Constable of Tynemouth and later Walsall was appointed in his stead. He became the second and last Chief Constable when the Borough Force was amalgamated with Dorset in 1967.

Donald Lockett, OBE, KPM, Chief Constable of Bournemouth.

The Lord Lieutenant and the Mayor of Bournemouth inspecting the Bournemouth contingent at a parade to celebrate the formation of the Dorset and Bournemouth Constabulary in 1967.

The Dorset and Bournemouth Constabulary

The amalgamation of the Dorset Constabulary and the Bournemouth Borough Police took place on October 1 1967. Arthur Hambleton was appointed Chief Constable with his Deputy being Walter Calverley and Donald Lockett becoming the Assistant Chief Constable.

The first Ford Anglia 'Panda' cars being paraded at Dorchester in 1967.

The Force establishment was made up of the 3 chief officers, 4 chief superintendents, 9 superintendents, 16 chief inspectors, 49 inspectors, 133 sergeants and 709 constables. The women on the Force consisted of one chief inspector, one inspector, 4 sergeants and 34 constables. Altogether there were 963 personnel. The Special Constabulary had a strength of 500.

Mr Graham Baker was appointed as the Chief Clerk, heading the 187 civilian staff. The strength of the traffic wardens had increased to 19 wardens. The Force was organised into three territorial divisions: Western Division, Central Division and Eastern Division (made up of the Borough of Bournemouth except for Kinson).

The sight of the 'bobby on the beat' became rarer when unit beat policing was introduced. First tried in Weymouth, it consisted of a residential beat officer working in a fixed area, assisted by a 'mobile officer with a conspicuously marked vehicle' with all officers equipped with personal radios. The experiment appeared successful and was extended to other parts of the county, and 6 Ford Anglia saloon cars were purchased as 'Panda Cars'. The following year, 29 vehicles were handed over by Colonel Weld, the Chairman of the Police Authority. Personal radios were also increased to a total of 145 sets. A new control room was opened with a vehicle display panel showing at a glance the number and situation of vehicles available for deployment.

Computers are Introduced

The basis of the car locator and recording scheme began early in 1964 by Detective Chief Superintendent Herbert Green when researching the possibility of using a computer to produce data as an aid to man management. At the time there had been no known similar studies in this field. A computer system, based upon Herbert Green's original research, for producing crime and traffic accident reports by grid locations, period and day, went into production on the 1st January 1965. In 1967, he was awarded a Winston Churchill Memorial Trust Fellowship, enabling him to visit the USA for six months to study crime prevention and detection, particularly with regard to the use of computers.

ABOVE The Dorset County Council computer section in 1965. The Force greatly relied on the County Council for computer services.

ABOVE RIGHT The American Express award certificate presented in 1969 along with 3,333 dollars.

In October 1969 the Chief Constable was, on behalf of the Force, presented with a prize of $3,333 by the IACP, an American Express Company, in Miami Beach, Florida, for devising the car locator scheme. This was part of $10,000 awarded annually for an outstanding contribution in the field of international police science and technology. In 1969 the award was shared with two police forces in the USA. The money was invested to set up the Force Scholarship Fund, providing the means each year for an officer to travel abroad and research such subjects as drugs in Columbia and missing children in Australia.

The 1965 system and the later 1969 system were submitted for the award, having been devised and written by Herbert Green in his own time. Mr K. Salter of the County Council computer section provided programming and technical advice.

The Force was also developing, at the same time, the first ever purpose-built police motorcycle. The Rickman 'Metisse' included in its specifications disc brakes, oil cooling through the frame and purpose built fairings and carrying equipment. The machine attracted world-wide interest with extensive press and television coverage. With some foresight the first press relations officer had been appointed the previous year.

Rural Beats

An experiment in rural policing was carried out in the Dorchester rural area. The eight former rural beats being policed by eight beat officers on motorcycles were replaced by patrols from Dorchester in two vans. Considered a success, it was adopted throughout the rest of the Force.

The loss of rural beat officers in villages ended the free service given by policemen's wives. PC Austin Crabb, who lived with his wife Pearl and family in the police house in

Constable Austin Crabb, the rural beat officer for Winfrith and the surrounding area.

The first *Alarm* launch in Weymouth Bay in 1971.

Winfrith, was the rural beat officer for an area stretching from Broadmayne to Lulworth. On one occasion while out patrolling on his motorcycle there was a knock on the door of the police office and on opening it Mrs Crabb was confronted by a 'rough, ugly-looking customer' who announced he was wanted by the police for burglary and had decided to give himself up. Mrs Crabb ushered him in and telephoned for help. She then detained the man as only a wife and mother could, by sitting him down in the kitchen and feeding him tea and cakes. Austin Crabb was to complain later that it was in fact his tea the man had eaten. Policemen's wives often took in lost property and acted as unpaid station desk officers. The demise of the village police house saw the loss of this valued free resource.

To save police manpower a policy had been adopted to employ more civilian staff. Since 1967 staff numbers had risen to 305 civilians including part-time staff and traffic wardens. The Special Constabulary were also doing their bit, the 451 members carried out a total of 21,538 hours of duty during 1970. Despite these savings, the introduction of a 40 hour week meant the practice of allowing officers time off for representative sport had to end.

Dogs were excluded from such restrictions and carried on competing. In 1971 the Force hosted the regional police dog trials and later in the year held the first internal force trials near Dorchester. Dog trials are a means of testing a dog's ability in subjects such as obedience, searching for objects, agility and following a track. Eight handlers and their dogs took part, the winner being PC Sparrey with his dog 'Russ'. Success had come to the Force dog section a few years earlier when Constable Colfer with 'Bruce' took part in the National Trials and became the National Police Dog Champion 1969.

Making a Splash

By the late 1960s Poole Harbour had approximately 5,000 craft within its shores. The need to police the Harbour rather more effectively led to a marine section being established and its first patrol boat being launched in April 1971 by Sir Joseph Weld. He named it *Alarm* after his great grandfather's sailing yacht, which had taken part in the first race now known as the 'America's Cup'. The launch, based on the Fairey 'Spearfish' sportboat, was

ABOVE Sergeant Colin Fagg and Constable Harry Vine were sent to Longbridge to take delivery of the first two Triumph 2000 patrol cars to be used in the country in 1968.

BELOW Coded Tone Generators were installed in patrol cars in 1972 to enable information to be sent to the Control Room regarding duties and location.

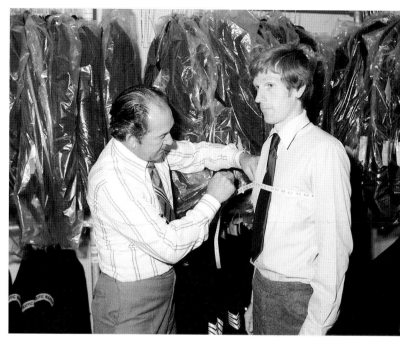

Mr Ray Roper, the Force tailor, fitting a new recruit with his uniform.

fitted with two 175 hp diesel engines giving a top speed of 30 knots. It was equipped with a 9ft dinghy with a 9.4hp outboard motor. Electronic light surveillance equipment enabled the launch to operate during darkness.

One of the more curious incidents in which the *Alarm* was involved in those early days took place when it was sent to a suspicious 'man-made' structure half way down the cliffs between St Alban's Head and Anvil Point. The shore unit was guided by loudhailer from the launch and when the shelter was reached it was found to house a Buddhist monk (complete with shrine and prayer mats) who had travelled from London seeking solitude. He was advised of the danger from cliff falls and took the advice and left to contemplate somewhere else.

In 1972 the Eastern Division control room was officially opened. Its features included the means for reception and automatic recording of data transmissions from vehicles in the form of a printout, illumination on a wall map and retrieval of the information displayed on visual display units at each console. This attracted considerable interest throughout the UK and overseas and by the end of the year there had been around 300 visits from people involved or interested in computerisation.

A month later there was a tragedy when a fire broke out in the recently refurbished Winfrith Ward at Coldharbour Hospital, Sherborne. The partitions constructed around

Along with other duties, rural patrol officers were expected to deal with problems such as rescuing dogs from drainpipes and herding cows back into their fields.

to protect visiting supporters from a minority of unruly home supporters. During two home matches at the start of the 1973/74 season, 54 supporters, including 40 juveniles, were arrested for breaches of the peace. Even Weymouth Football Club felt the need to double the police presence at matches, despite each constable costing the club £6.50. Offences of 'violence against the person' rose by 111 over the previous year to 530. Serious woundings and assaults also rose by an unprecedented 120 to a total of 510.

An example of this type of violent crime happened in Bournemouth when an 18 year old girl walking through King's Park was, for no apparent reason, viciously attacked by a man who struck her over the head several times with an iron bar. Her screams were heard by two young boys aged eight and nine who saw the assault. The boys ran to the scene and when the man saw them he made off on a pedal cycle and, although pursued by one of the boys, escaped. The other boy comforted the girl and arranged for the police to be called. Following extensive enquiries a man was arrested for the offence and later sentenced to five years imprisonment. At the end of the case the judge awarded the two boys £10 each in recognition of their actions and bravery and they later appeared on Southern ITV's Crime Desk where they were each presented them with a cheque from the girl's father.

A happily more lighthearted story involved PC John Hogan, who with other officers had been called to a flat in Bournemouth in 1973 to deal with an incident involving a mental patient and a dog, both being taken away. Afterwards PC Hogan realised he had locked his helmet inside the flat. After his colleagues had found an open kitchen window they pushed the constable, with great difficulty, through the small window – where he fell into the refuse bucket. By then his fellow officers realised he was in the wrong flat, but their frantic signals were ignored. The rather smelly constable made his way out of the kitchen and into the lounge, where an elderly couple were sitting by the fire.

Constable Hogan, unperturbed, said 'Good evening.'

The elderly couple replied 'Good evening.'

John Hogan tried to explain his presence by saying, 'I am a police officer,' obviously apologising for lack of

the beds to provide a sense of privacy led to great difficulty in evacuating the 36 mentally subnormal patients sleeping in the dormitory, of whom 30 died from asphyxiation. After a major investigation into the circumstances surrounding these deaths the Director of Public Prosecutions advised that there was insufficient evidence for any criminal proceedings.

In 1973 hooliganism was reported as 'continuing unabated . . . the exuberance of youth cannot excuse the inconvenience caused to private citizens'. Although British Rail introduced trains especially for soccer fans, this itself caused problems in Bournemouth in that it was necessary headgear.

The elderly lady replied 'How nice of you to drop in, we would like to complain about a dog.'

The constable told them he had dealt with that matter and as they were alright he would be going.

The gentleman then said, 'Thank you again for dropping in. Anytime you are passing come in. Good night.'

A relieved John Hogan left quietly by the front door.

Not quite so relieved, except for a £20 fine, was PC Huw Glover who while driving back to the Weymouth Police Station after spending the day pointing a 'Radar gun' at motorists, collided with another car, which he then bounced off before ramming the front of a Range Rover. The Range Rover's driver, a naval officer, immediately got out and asked if anyone was injured. To his horror, PC Glover found himself face to face with the Prince of Wales, who was returning to East Dorset, where he was staying while attending a course at Portland. Huw Glover, although making headlines, was never asked to be part of the Royal Protection Squad – nor was he thought to have been responsible for the name of the Force to change the following year from the Dorset and Bournemouth Constabulary to Dorset Police.

A Rickman Metisse machine developed as a purpose built motorcycle by the Force.

NINE

The Dorset Police

ON 1ST APRIL 1974 local Government reorganisation enlarged the county of Dorset to include Bournemouth, Christchurch and the parishes of Hurn, St Leonards and St Ives. At the end of 1974 the establishment of the Force was 3 chief officers, 4 chief superintendents, 14 superintendents, 21 chief inspectors, 158 sergeants and 776 constables.

Policewomen were still counted separately and had a strength of one superintendent, one chief inspector, 2 inspectors, 8 sergeants and 52 constables. Susan Gospel, who had transferred from Cambridgeshire, became the first woman superintendent to be appointed in the county

The Women's Hockey Team reached the final of the National Policewomen's Hockey Competition in 1976. The team were Jane Lee, Karen Mack, Wendy Brooks, Lyn Cresswell, Liz Eastick, Pam Booth, Jill Spooner, Margaret Constandinos, Denise Jones, Alison Gracie, Terry Sparshot, and Sue Gospel. Bill Hall trained them.

Force. Shortly afterwards women's pay was brought into line with men's, previously it had been 10% less. In the following year the Sex Discrimination Act was introduced, bringing an end to all discrimination. Supporting the uniformed force were 273 whole time and 30 part-time civilian staff, 64 traffic wardens and 32 seasonal traffic wardens.

The *Blueprint*, a Force newspaper, was introduced in the same year (it is still being produced in 2006, although in magazine form). In the first edition the Chief Constable, Mr Hambleton wrote:

> Minority groups are close knit, united, and have a common purpose; their espirit de corps and dedication ensure that their successes are greater than their numbers would normally achieve. The Police Service of this country is a minority group – in England and Wales, the population is approximately fifty million with 10,000 police officers; the newly enlarged Dorset will have a population of 560,000 and 1,100 police officers.
>
> The undoubted success which the police service has enjoyed over the years is, in part, due to the same reasons that minority groups in other spheres have fulfilled their aims. It is with a spirit of unity, a common aim, and an intention to serve the public to the utmost degree that the new Dorset Police has been founded.'

New Technology

To discover how the Force computer project could be enhanced the Police Scientific Development Branch of the Home Office sent Dr Michael Smart and Superintendent Gerald Openshaw to carry out a study. The project, known as the Management Information System (MIS), was led by Superintendent Victor Wilcox. After a formal presentation at the Home Office, an offer was made of financial support and of the help and expertise of a team of scientists conditional on the Police Committee providing the hardware necessary to develop the system. With much foresight the Police Committee agreed, and the project was formally launched.

Technological breakthroughs were becoming second nature to the Force. One such example was the installation of the first permanent optical fibre link in Britain in the Control Room in Bournemouth by Standard Telephones and Cables Ltd in conjunction with the Home Office. The cable provided a 10 megabit per second data link between the digital core store beneath the Control Room and the visual display units in the Control Room.

This new technology was attracting attention and among the visitors during 1974 was the Minister of State at the Home Office, Lord Harris. Other visitors came from Israel, Iran, Australia, Hong Kong, Ethiopia, Nigeria, Bermuda, Malaysia and Canada. A less welcome visitor was a lightning strike in September, which hit the aerial at Bournemouth Police Station and caused considerable damage to the electronic equipment in the Control Room.

Dual computers were installed in Bournemouth to ensure the reliability essential in a police operational system and 31 visual display units (VDUs) were purchased. The computer system was demonstrated to UK Chief Officers and overseas delegates attending an International Symposium on Police Technology – an exhibition staged jointly by the Electronic Engineering Association and the Home Office at Wembley Conference Centre. The Plessey Company stand included two VDU terminals and a hard copy printer directly linked into the mini computer at Bournemouth, enabling delegates to see live incident logging and message switching. The Force was represented by Victor Wilcox, his successor, Superintendent Leonard Chick, and Sergeants Hinchliffe and Pomeroy.

What had not seen before in Dorset was 'streaking'. The Force warned that offenders would be 'streaking' straight into trouble if caught. Although a 'well-built and suntanned all over' man – according to astonished eye-witnesses – who dashed up East Street in Wimborne before disappearing into the car park of the Rising Sun pub did not get caught, 'Tattooed Terry' and a 17 year old girl were arrested for a breach of the peace and fined £20.

The year of the Queen's Silver Jubilee in 1977 had begun with the Chief Constable being awarded the CBE in the New Year's Honours list. A ceremony in tribute to the Queen was held at the Metropolitan Police Training Centre at Hendon attended by 3,000 police officers, traffic wardens, police cadets, civilian staff, special constables, members of police authorities and their wives. The 24 strong Dorset contingent was headed by Assistant Chief Constable Leonard Burt and included Superintendent Peter Hoper, Constable Tony Beale and Special Chief Superintendent Colin Coles. All three were presented to the Queen, and all three had been prisoners of war – Colin Coles and Tony Beale by the Japanese and Peter Hoper by the Chinese communists in North Korea. Constable Austin Crabb represented the Dorset Police in the Guard of Honour.

In March, the Deputy Chief Constable, Dennis Habgood died after a short illness. Dennis Habgood was 56 and had occupied the post since 1973. At his funeral 250 police officers led by the Chief Constable marched ahead of the hearse from the King's Statue to St Joseph's Church in Weymouth. The Chief Constable in his address said 'Dennis Habgood was a patriot, a gentleman, and a policeman. He loved his country very dearly, serving as a navigator in the RAF during the war. He served the police nationally when he went away from home for three years to direct the Command Courses at the Police College. He gave all his leisure hours – what little he had – to St John Ambulance.'

Drought, Blizzards & the move to Winfrith

The abnormally dry hot weather throughout the spring and summer of 1976 resulted in large areas of parched forests and heathlands being turned into raging infernos by the many serious fires. Over 9,000 acres of hedgerow, heathland, forest and private property were destroyed as flames fanned by high winds raced through the vegetation at speeds approaching 20mph. In one blaze 360 geriatric patients were evacuated from St Leonards Hospital in the path of the advancing fire. Another serious fire at Winfrith spread over the heath so rapidly the Fire Brigade could not

A fire in 1975 coming very close to the Petroleum Depot at West Moors.

contain it. Although people and animals were evacuated safely, some farm buildings were destroyed.

The cliff rescue team were stood down after eleven years of service and HM Coastguard assumed responsibility. They had made many rescues, such as the couple, unknown to each other at the time, who met by chance when climbing on Ballard Cliff near Swanage. Unfortunately they fell and received serious injuries but after recovering, having decided they made a good team became man and wife. Animals were also rescued. When an in-calf cow fell over the cliffs at Eype, the team were called out and lowered a vet down to tranquillize the cow which was then lifted off the cliff face by a Royal Naval helicopter. Word was later received that mother and son were doing well.

The Constabulary Headquarters in Dorchester near Maumbury Rings had for some time been inadequate. The original buildings had been designed as living accommodation. Although two portakabins had been erected in the middle of the yard, neither the original buildings nor the portakabins provided the necessary space for a modern police force. After attempting to find a site in Dorchester without success, a building and 8 acres of land became available at Winfrith when the Dragon project, a European Nuclear research programme, was closed down. Although there were plans to build a purpose-built headquarters in later years, the move from Dorchester to Winfrith in November 1977 was to the buildings as they then stood. These have since been extended in phases to include a Control Room, restaurant, training building and stores. The old headquarters became the Western Division Headquarters until the new one was opened in Weymouth, and it is now Dorchester Police Station.

ABOVE After nearly 120 years of serving as the Force Headquarters the flag was lowered for the last time in 1977 and the headquarters was removed to Winfrith. The Dorchester buildings became the Western Divisional Headquarters until they in turn moved to Weymouth in 2000. The front part of the original buildings are still being used as the Dorchester Police Station.

BELOW Newly supplied Ford Cortinas and Escorts arranged in front of the new headquarters at Winfrith.

1978 started off with blizzard conditions, on the 19th February every road within the county was blocked by snow. Rail links were closed and electricity and water supplies were cut off to thousands of homes. To allow snow clearance work to proceed unhindered the Chief Constable took the unprecedented step of banning all vehicles from the roads.

Former Wimborne policeman, Brian Lush, describes his experiences:

'On the Sunday morning I had just moved to the new police station in Wimborne when I received a call from Dr William Russell. He had been asked to attend a 15 year-old boy who had an acute appendicitis and lived at an isolated house in Merley Park.

After talking to Station Officer Dick Farrance, we decided the only way we could get there with the doctor would be by using the Fire Service's Landrover. On reaching Merley, even in a 4-wheel drive vehicle, it was obvious the main road was as far as we could go, so Dr Russell decided to go it alone and took off on his skis for the house.

Soon after, the boy's father arrived with a JCB digger and we climbed aboard – all eight of us – and drove a mile to the house where the doctor was contemplating performing the operation

on the kitchen table. However, after second thoughts a makeshift stretcher was made from two boat oars and some settee seats. The lad was put into three or four sleeping bags, fitted with a woolly hat, and step by step we carried him to the main road through 8ft snow drifts, a totally exhausting journey, where a Range Rover 4-wheel ambulance took him to Poole General Hospital for his operation.

During the four days Dorset was cut off from the outside world by the "living white hell", as the Chief Constable called it, the police station in Wimborne remained open and I worked and slept there. But I wasn't alone as some of the crew of the old *Ark Royal* who were due back in Plymouth, were also stranded, so they kept me company before eventually catching a specially arranged train from Salisbury. During this time we were being fed by the kind people of Wimborne who struggled through the snow to bring us food. I will never forget their hospitality and many kindnesses during the time I was privileged to serve them as their community 'Bobby'.'

The snow soon melted and 1978 turned into a busy year. In April the Force hosted the 20th National Champion Police Dog Trials at Blandford Army Camp. Later in the year the first Family Day was held at Winfrith for members of the Force and their families and in October over 5,000 people attended a road safety day at the Pier Approach in Bournemouth.

Such events did much to help the relationship between the police and the public, but a more private tribute was the one paid to two recently retired officers by Judge Pennant, who sat at Dorchester, by saying to the lawyers and court officials present, 'We are privileged to have in court this morning two very well-known and distinguished Dorset people; Mr Anthony Michael Beale and Mr Ronald Harry Beale. They were better known for many years as police officers of the Dorset Force, and as such they conducted themselves so outstandingly well that they commanded, I believe, the respect and affection of almost every section of the public.'

Firearms Incidents

In 1978 an investigation had begun into alleged corruption in the Metropolitan Police led by Dorset's Deputy Chief Constable, Leonard Burt. The enquiry, later named 'Operation Countryman', resulted in a great many officers being away from Dorset at the investigation base in Goldaming. The enquiry eventually resulted in the imprisonment of the Flying Squad's Chief Superintendent and twelve other detectives and the resignation of many more officers. The idea of one of the smallest country forces investigating the largest caused some humour, and in some quarters the team became known, not as the Sweeny, but the 'Sweedy'.

In June a serious incident took place when Sergeant Stroud and Constable Drew were sent to a school in Bournemouth as a result of an alarm being activated. Two men were spotted climbing out a window and running away in opposite directions. PC Drew chased after one of them who turned and shot the officer in the leg with a revolver. Sgt Stroud pursued the same man and was also shot at without being hit. Although the men escaped they were later arrested. They admitted stealing chemicals to make explosive powder for ammunition for the revolver and were found to be in possession of a large number of guns, knives and other offensive weapons. The offender who used the revolver was sent to prison for nine years and his accomplice for six years. PC Drew, after recovering in hospital returned to duty later in the year. The following June he was awarded the Queen's Gallantry Medal and Sgt Stroud was commended by Her Majesty for Brave Conduct.

There was concern when a second shooting incident happened shortly afterwards. Constables Newland and Ferry were in pursuit of a car reported to have been stolen from Bristol. The vehicle, sometimes reaching a speed of 100mph was followed from Dorchester to Weymouth and then towards Wool. It contained two men and a woman. At East Knighton the car was forced to stop at roadworks and the two men got out of the car armed with shotguns. The two police officers and Constable Green, a third officer who had just arrived at the scene, were ordered to leave their vehicles and forced to lie on the ground. Three gunshots were fired, one of which hit a tyre of the patrol car. Another hit the ground about 12 inches in front of PC Newland causing serious injuries to his face.

The assailants made off in the stolen car which they

On Parade

The highlight of 1979 was undoubtedly the visit by the Queen and Duke of Edinburgh to the Eastern Division Control Room in Bournemouth where they inspected the Force computerised command and control system. They were accompanied by the Lord Lieutenant and shown around by the Chief Constable, Chief Superintendent Royston Scott and Superintendent Leonard Chick, the Force Computer Projects Officer. During their tour the development of the computerised command and control systems was explained and they were shown demonstrations of the system from operational activities in progress at the time, including the logging, updating and

Constable Allan Drew outside Buckingham Palace in 1978 after receiving the Queen's Gallantry Medal.

Her Majesty The Queen and the Chief Constable leaving Bournemouth Police Station after visiting the Control Room.

abandoned at Lulworth. An operation involving trained firearms officers and a military helicopter was mounted and the offenders were eventually arrested on the gunnery ranges at Lulworth after throwing their weapons and ammunition into the sea. Two shotguns and 50 cartridges were recovered later by a Royal Marine diving team. The offenders appeared at Dorchester Crown Court where one man was sentenced to 10 years imprisonment, the other to eight years and the woman was placed on probation for three years.

Chief Constable David Owen, QPM.

officer, but I regret to say in this day and age, when we have to be cost-effective, when manpower is at a premium, when technology has brought the era of the instant response, I have to look long and hard to find the resources and to employ them in the most meaningful manner for the benefit of the community at large.'

Chief Constable Owen, in his first annual report commented: 'To my mind, little is achieved by the quick easy answer from the self-appointed expert. Restoration of capital or corporal punishment as the complete panacea for all ills is not in my view the answer. What is required is a concerted effort from all in support of law and order.'

He went on to mention a recent comment in the Queen's Bench Division that 'vandalism, violence, excessive noise, disorder and indecent behaviour has been rife later at night

Col Sir Joseph Weld inspecting the 125th anniversary parade.

monitoring of incidents and the allocation of resources to deal with them.

Later in the year a Church Parade was held to mark the forthcoming retirement of Colonel Sir Joseph Weld as Chairman of the Dorset Police Committee. He had been a member of the committee since 1953 and its Chairman since 1960. Major General Mark Bond replaced him as Chairman.

At the end of February 1980, the Chief Constable, Arthur Hambleton also retired. Replacing Arthur Hambleton was David Owen, previously the Deputy Chief Constable of Merseyside Police. Born in Betws-y-Coed, North Wales, he joined the Metropolitan Police in 1951 where he served in the CID until being appointed Assistant Chief Constable of Lincolnshire Police.

In a speech to the Dorset Association of Local Councils at Dorchester David Owen said that under no circumstances could there ever be a return of the village bobby. 'The village policeman, regrettably, is a matter of history. I am fully wedded to the concept of the foot patrol

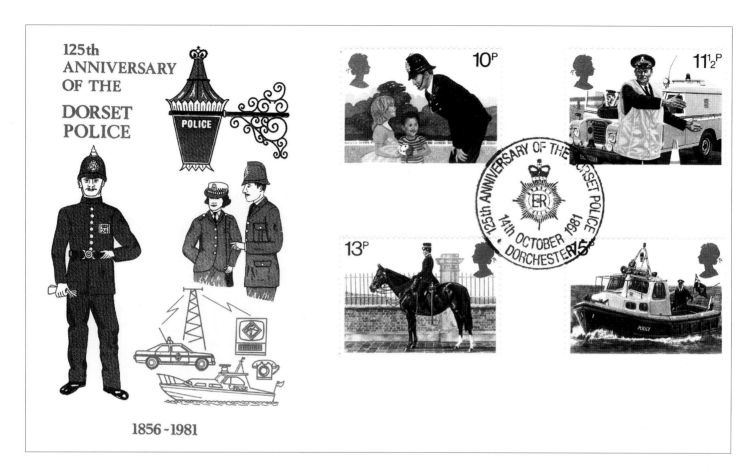

125th
ANNIVERSARY
OF THE
DORSET
POLICE

POLICE

1856-1981

10P

11½P

13P

and in the early hours of the morning in central Bournemouth during 1980 and particularly so in Glen Fern Road and Old Christchurch Road area.' He added, 'if people persist in wishing to turn this area into a mini-Soho, they are going the right way about it. It is really a matter for the populace of Bournemouth – if you want a mini-Soho, then don't expect the police, based on a county establishment, to maintain public tranquillity at all times.'

Drug abuse was also a continuing concern. In 1979 four deaths occurred, in 1980 this had doubled to eight, all of them being between 20 and 29 years of age. The quantity of illegal drugs in circulation can be understood by an incident in September when a man walking his dog along

The first day cover issued to celebrate the 125th anniversary of the Dorset Police.

Studland beach found several sacks of cannabis resin partly hidden in the sand. A total of 72 sacks were eventually unearthed, weighing a total of 2,175kg. Despite a watch being kept no one came to collect them.

The 125th anniversary of county policing in Dorset was marked in September by a parade and church service in Dorchester. Almost 200 men and women took part in the parade. In October 1981 a commemorative First Day Cover stamp was issued, 125 years after the first Chief Constable was appointed in 1856.

TEN

Upholding the Law

THE EARLY 1980s were troubled times, and the Force was requested to provide aid to Toxteth, Merseyside and Leicestershire following a dramatic escalation in inner city rioting. With little need, previously, for equipment to deal with riots, 200 NATO style anti-riot helmets had to be quickly purchased and Transit personnel carriers fitted with homemade grills to protect their windscreens.

A very different concern was the always unpredictable English weather. On December 13 1981 heavy snow started to fall in Dorset, accompanied by strong winds and abnormally high tides, with a warning of flooding at West Bay and Portland. During the morning four-wheel-drive vehicles from the Dorset County Council were allocated to various stations. In the afternoon a chaotic situation developed and there was widespread electricity supply failures. The computer in the control room went down and was not restored until the next morning, radio communications also became difficult. Electricity and telephone lines were brought down, fallen trees blocked roads. Automatic alarm systems were activated due to loss of power and vehicles were stuck in snow drifts. An emergency centre was opened at Castlefield School in Dorchester where food, drink and shelter was provided for approximately 200 people brought to safety from cars stuck in snowdrifts on the A35 between Bridport and Dorchester.

By daylight conditions had improved dramatically and people in the reception centre were able to be returned to their vehicles and to resume their journeys. During the storms two young men lost their lives – one died of hypothermia attempting to secure a boat in Poole Harbour and the other was washed off the Cobb in Lyme Regis by a freak wave.

There was change at the top when David Owen was appointed as the Chief Constable of North Wales after only two years with Dorset. He was replaced by Brian Weight, previously Deputy Chief Constable of Bedfordshire, who took up his appointment in June 1982.

In 1984 bicycles were still being used, along with capes and radios.

Chief Constable Brian Weight, QPM.

The new Chief Constable set up two new departments, an Operations Department responsible for among others, firearms, the dog section, marine section and police support unit training. The second department – Community Relations – was responsible for crime prevention, and among other tasks organised the county youth adventure camp on Dartmoor and the police section of the Duke of Edinburgh Award Scheme.

Trouble at football matches in Bournemouth at Dean Court was again making headlines. The first incident was in January 1984 when AFC Bournemouth played Manchester United in the FA Cup before a crowd of 15,600. Just before the end of the match a number of away supporters left the Brighton Beach end of the ground and ran to the south stand occupied by the home supporters. Scuffles broke out and a surge in the crowd caused five crash barriers to collapse. Fortunately there were no serious injuries.

In May Bournemouth played Millwall FC. About 600 visiting fans attended the match and were disorderly throughout, invading the pitch twice. After the match there was trouble and shop windows were broken. In November, Millwall were drawn away to Weymouth in the FA Cup and with their record of violence an operation involving 150 regulars and specials was mounted to police the match: even so, 14 people were arrested.

Public order policing was becoming a regular occurrence. From March, support units performed duties outside the Force area in connection with miner's disputes in North and South Yorkshire, Leicestershire, Nottinghamshire, Warwickshire and Kent. The officers were deployed on 36 occasions with a total of 150 Police Support Units made up of 3,312 officers plus 25 liaison officers. (A support consists of an inspector, 3 sergeants

Chief Inspector Geoffrey Bartlett, liaison officer with the working miners during the 1985 miners' strike with a miner's lamp, helmet and knee protectors presented to him.

Constable Clive Chamberlain with Olive the singing parrot appeared on the television programme 'That's Life' in the late 1980s.

and 18 constables). Most of the units travelled on a Sunday and returned on the Friday following. The hours worked always consisted of 12 hour working days, mostly between midnight and 12 noon. The Chief Constable reported that when he visited his officers in South Yorkshire he saw them returning from a 14 hour shift, grey-faced and exhausted but nevertheless cheerful and determined. The miners' strike continued to March 1985. It took its strain on the Force, with a tenth of constables working outside Dorset.

A campaign was launched in 1985 to inform people about the dangers of drug misuse. A series of meetings was held throughout the county where films, video presentations and lectures were given to the public and at each meeting a talk was given by a young person heavily addicted to hard drugs. The video included messages from pop stars and sportsmen. Over 5,000 people attended these meetings and officers also visited schools and youth clubs

and spoke to over 100,000 school children and young people. An amnesty was offered to drug addicts who approached the police and asked for help or informed on their suppliers. This brought about the arrest of 203 drug suppliers. The campaign was financed by money raised by sponsorship under the guidance of Peter Allesbrook, the President of the Dorset Chamber of Commerce and Industry, who raised donations totalling £5,000.

The Labour Party conference was held in Bournemouth at the beginning of October 1985. Sergeant Maurice Barrett and his team at the main entrance set out to prove the friendliness of the Dorset Force by adopting a warm and courteous manner to all the delegates. Their smiles and daily greetings soon began to make an impression and the delegates, even the more militant such as Arthur Scargill and Derek Hatton, were soon offering friendly banter. One delegate exclaimed, 'I have been amazed, I have never seen so many smiling policemen in all of my life, I just cannot understand it!' At the end of the conference the chairman proposed a vote of thanks to the police, the first occasion this had ever happened, and a recognition that it was the Dorset Police who initiated the healing process between the Labour Party and the Police in the wake of the Miners' Strike.

Weymouth Community Constable Clive Chamberlain also made an impression during the conference when he appeared on Noel Edmunds 'Late, Late Breakfast Show' giving his impersonation of Sir Robin Day. This wetted his appetite for fame, and a few years later he appeared on Esther Rantzen's 'That's Life' with Olive, a parrot, sitting on his shoulder singing while he played the piano.

Challenging Times

The year 1986 was, according to Brian Weight, the most challenging year in the history of the Dorset Police service – the year of the introduction of modern computer and communication technology, and the biggest and most demanding police operation mounted in the county at Bournemouth International Centre.

1986 also saw the introduction of the Police and Criminal Evidence Act (PACE), which brought about many complicated changes to the criminal law. The bureaucracy necessary to comply with the provision of the Act was considerable and inhibited the questioning of prisoners as compared to previous practice, introducing recording equipment and soundproofed interview rooms.

Further legislation created the Crown Prosecution Service. A Crown Prosecutor was appointed who became responsible for prosecutions in Dorset and Hampshire. Previously each Force had a Principle Prosecuting Solicitor as well as inspectors prosecuting in Magistrate's Courts.

In May, a 'Hippy Convoy' descended on the county from Somerset. It required an escort of 350 police officers from Dorset, Devon and Cornwall, Avon and Somerset, Wiltshire and Hampshire, and the convoy reached Wytch on the Studland road after confrontations with the residents of Ringstead. The next day it moved on towards Ashley Heath and then on to Stoney Cross. Along the route police vehicles were rammed and 20 people arrested. Later, over 100 Dorset officers assisted Hampshire Constabulary to evict them from Forestry Commission land at Stoney Cross.

In July a new force Control Room at Winfrith took over from the control room in Dorchester. The HOLMES (Home Office Large Major Enquiry System) software package designed to control the investigation of major crimes was supplied to the Force. In exchange, the supplying software house used the Force as a reference site for other forces interested in purchasing the package.

In October the security for the policing of the Conservative Party Conference in Bournemouth at the BIC was greatly heightened following the IRA bomb which killed five people and injured 30 at the Grand Hotel in Brighton the previous year. The size of the operation far outstripped the resources of the force and reinforcements from nine other forces were required. The 1,000 officers were accommodated at a holiday camp and hotels in Bournemouth.

Of the seven murders during the year the biggest enquiry was into the death of Sandra Court, whose strangled body was found in a water-filled ditch alongside Avon Causeway near Christchurch. The statistics into this murder enquiry, which is still undetected, illustrate the work involved in a major investigation: 2,018 telephone calls were made,

One of the 'Hippy Convoys' that caused trouble in 1986.

11,500 enquiries investigated, 4,300 statements taken from 3,686 people, 5,000 sets of fingerprints taken and a total of 61,782 man hours devoted to the enquiry.

Early in 1987 new main VHF equipment was installed at all four hilltop sites as a prelude to conversion of mobile VHF sets. This programme was part of changes resulting

With the increase in size of Verwood a new 24-hour Panda patrol was started in May 1987. They were Constables Ian Blanchett, Dave Scott, Andy Brockway and Les Jeffery with Inspector Mike Nunn in the car.

The fast response urban patrol in front of the Customs House, Poole in 1990.

from the World Administrative Radio Conference (WARC) for police and emergency services generally. With the withdrawal of rented radios from the Home Office the force was required to buy 2,000 Motorola radios.

It was a busy year operationally. In June, 3,500 residents in Poole had to be evacuated after a fire at the British Drug Houses Factory. The fire spread rapidly to where chemicals and chemical liquid were stored. A large fireball enveloped the area as drums of chemical liquid and debris were propelled into the air, many of which landed outside the premises in West Street. There were no fatalities, although the occupants of a burning car were lucky to escape. Poole Arts Centre became the reception centre for those who were evacuated from their homes.

Hippies and drunkenness were again a problem. Twenty

constables were sent to Stonehenge to assist Wiltshire Constabulary police the 5,000 'hippy' travellers in the area. Even a town as seemingly quiet as Wareham witnessed a disturbance (described as a riot in one Sunday paper) after a man was arrested near the Horse and Groom. Twenty officers from Weymouth, Poole, Blandford and Swanage were involved in running battles with youths, in which three officers were injured and six men arrested.

The CID was hit hard with three murder inquiries within a week. Although a man surrendered himself to a police officer in the first case, extensive enquiries were carried out in the other two cases. A computerised murder incident room was established for the first time in the county after Samuel Williamson was discovered dead after a severe beating at the rear of the DHSS offices in Christchurch Road, Bournemouth.

The other case was that of a missing nine year old, Tiffany Hoiles in Blandford. Incidents involving children affect everyone and it is not hard to obtain the help of the public. Following an extensive search, her pedal cycle was found and later also her body near the old railway line path in the area known as Milldown. Aided by a great deal of local intelligence, a Blandford man was arrested and later charged with the murder. Forensic science was successfully used to connect pieces of string taken from various locations and linked to the accused, to identify body fluids and to compare fibre evidence. The man was sentenced to life imprisonment.

A new event for Dorset happened in 1989 when the first 'acid house party' was held in Bournemouth attended by 3,000 young people. Complaints were made regarding noise, the availability of illegal drugs and alcohol – perhaps the cause of the violence shown to officers. 'Positive' action had to be taken in the early hours, requiring the use of short riot shields for the first time in the county.

At the end of the year the ambulance service was involved in a strike. A request was made by the Health Authority for assistance, and three police personnel carriers were converted into temporary ambulances. By December 15 a total of 11 police vehicles had been converted, each crewed by a traffic patrol driver and a

Police Support Unit training was made more realistic and necessary in the 1990s.

when, despite warnings from the Chief Constable, the Football League authorities allowed a game between Bournemouth AFC and Leeds United to go ahead. The Leeds supporters came to Bournemouth in great numbers and could not all get into the ground. Officers came under severe and sustained attack, both at the ground and in the town centre. One officer was hit by a large piece of masonry and was taken unconscious to hospital. At the height of the disturbance, 19 Police Support Units from Dorset, Hampshire, Wiltshire, Gloucester and Avon and Somerset as well as the mounted section of the City of London Police were used outside the football ground to control the marauding Leeds supporters.

Leeds United football team supporters came to Bournemouth in great numbers in August 1991. Not being able to get into the Dean Park stadium, they caused trouble both at the ground and in the town.

divisional officer. Four days later eight military ambulances and their crews were deployed with a police liaison officer attached to each. ACC Alan Rose later said, 'there has been little informed comment about the magnificent response by soldiers, police officers and police civilians who worked long hours under trying circumstances with inadequate transport and resources. It should be appreciated that they did not volunteer for the job, neither did they, in most cases, want to do it, but they are members of disciplined organisations who are ensuring the sick and injured of Dorset are taken to hospital when the need arises. Who else would have done it?'

Another major investigation involving a child was launched in August 1990 when seven year old Gemma Lawrence was abducted through a caravan window at West Bay whilst she was sleeping. Hundreds of holidaymakers, local residents, soldiers and police searched for her from Sunday until she was finally found, alive and well, in a hut in an overgrown garden. Her abductor, was later made the subject of an order under the Mental Health Act.

Public Order training for which officers volunteered proved its usefulness during the Bank Holiday weekend

Sergeant John Walsh and Police Dog Otto who beat 30 other teams to become National Police Dogs Trials Champion. Constable Alan Buswell is holding one of two pups Otto fathered after his success.

OPPOSITE PAGE TOP Conference Point 1992, a reconstruction of the first Conference Point shown on page 19. Standing left to right: Chief Superintendents David Trickey, John Homer, Bill Hanson, Des Donohoe, David Russell, John Elliott. Sitting ACO Peter Lewis, DCC Tony Pointer, CC Brian Weight and ACC Alan Rose.

OPPOSITE PAGE BOTTOM The Bournemouth Beat Team in 1993. Left to right: Constables Ray Beswick, Chris Mason, Dave Williams, Ken Atkins, Keith Bunn, Dave Evans, Supt Jim Power, Constables Howard Bailey, Peter Wright, Verity Bonwitt, Jill Durham, Malcolm Warriner and Sergeant Charlie Eggar.

In April 1991, Jo Ramsden, who suffered from Down's Syndrome, was reported missing from Bridport. Six days of extensive searching followed. 'It was an excellent response from the public,' said Superintendent Thornley, 'It showed what a really caring community Bridport is.' Her body was eventually found in woodland near Lyme Regis. A man was later charged with her murder along with various cases of rape of mentally disturbed women. Although convicted of the rapes, the charge of murder was found not to be conclusive and was left on file. The man, a former nurse, was sent to Broadmoor for life.

Major General Bond retired as Chairman of the Police Authority in 1992. He had been its Chairman for 12 years and a member for 18. Sir Stephen Hammick, who succeeded him made a plea to parents: 'Please do all you can to bring up your children to respect the law . . . All too often the police officers we ask to uphold the law are attacked for their pain. Surely such a response, apart from bringing retribution on the offenders, must also bring shame and a sense of guilt to parents who cannot, or will not, control their children.'

On Track

Sergeant John Walsh and Police Dog Otto beat 30 other teams at the National Police Dog Trials to become National Champion 1991.

Another well known police dog was 'Max' who along with handler Constable Alan Lowe, was awarded the 'Police Dog Action of the Year 1992' national award. The award was for an incident when the team were called to the scene of a hit and run accident in the early hours of the morning. Max soon picked up the trail of the three offenders, leading to a seven mile cross country chase in darkness along a country lane, through a private garden, on through farmyards and into open fields. One field contained a herd of cows, but nevertheless Max held to the scent until three men were seen walking away in the distance. Poor radio communications had not enabled any backup to be called, so PC Lowe ordered the offenders to lie down immediately on the ground. With loud barking from Max they reluctantly did so. All three were arrested. Max, with a reputation as an enthusiastic dog, had contributed to over 300 arrests over five years.

The year 1993 was another full of incident, including terrorism in Bournemouth. A number of explosions and incendiary devices were planted on Bournemouth Pier and in six shops, one device in a furniture shop caused extensive damage – altogether the damage was estimated at £1 million. The IRA were suspected of planting them. Firearms were used on 56 occasions by criminals and armed police were employed on 26 occasions. This led to the introduction of an armed response vehicle, a car operated by trained firearms officers and carrying weapons.

The cameras of the BBC's 'Crimewatch' television programme reconstructed a serious crime that had occurred in Poole. PCs Charlie Dale and Steve Hogarth were called to the United Dairies premises at Fleetsbridge where an armed robbery had taken place. Two of three robbers, who were armed with shotguns, threatened a young woman cashier and escaped with £8,000. The officers, trying to stop the getaway car, pulled up just ahead of it. One of the robbers, who was wearing an 'old man' mask, thrust a shotgun out of the car window and fired at the policemen from a range of five yards. Luckily both officers escaped serious injury but had to have surgery in Poole and Weymouth.

Another armed robbery took place at a post office in Hamworthy. The robbers, who stole £20,000, were armed with a shotgun and a crowbar. A customer who attempted to stop them escaping was shot twice at point-blank range and although having to spend a long time in hospital eventually recovered. Two men were later imprisoned for the offences. Later in the year in the same area Constables George and Mallace was shot at when patrolling the Turlin Moor Estate and although a bullet pierced their car neither officer was injured.

Children were again involved in two tragic incidents. Inspector Mason, PCs Elsdon, Harris, Lavin and Hester were awarded the Queen's Commendation for Brave Conduct for their part in an incident in which a man had doused his two young children in petrol and threatened to kill himself and them. After a high speed car chase, manoeuvering and stopping the car, the children were rescued and the man arrested.

Another horrible incident occurred when four Devon schoolchildren on an adventure holiday at a Lyme Regis centre were drowned whilst canoeing in West Bay. Shortly after 10am a party of eight pupils, one teacher and two instructors from the Southway Comprehensive School in Plymouth set out from the beach at Lyme Regis. The party got into difficulties, after an instructor and teacher became separated from the main party, and all were blown away from the shore.

Although due to reach Charmouth by lunchtime nothing was seen of the party and nothing reported until a fisherman found an empty canoe. Two helicopters from Portland Naval air base were scrambled, later joined by a helicopter from RAF Chivenor in north Devon, the helicopter of HMS *Beaver* and the inshore lifeboat from Lyme Regis. By late afternoon the lifeboat had found two adults suffering from hypothermia. The Sea King picked up another canoeist followed by three others. Shortly afterwards the RAF Wessex helicopter reported picking up four more. Finally the Sea King picked up the last canoeist, who was still breathing, nearly nine hours after they had set off. They were all taken to Weymouth Hospital.

The Managing Director of the Outdoor Leisure activities company was convicted on four counts of manslaughter at Winchester Crown Court and was sentenced to a total of three years imprisonment. The company became the first limited company in the country to be convicted of corporate manslaughter. Detective Constable Roger Mutch, the liaison officer to the families, was recognised for his work when he was invited to 10 Downing Street to meet Prime Minister John Major.

The Unexpected

A 50 year old German visitor caused a great upheaval in Portland. The 1,100lb bomb dropped during the Second World War was discovered on the old football ground in Grove Road in 1994. It triggered a massive operation in which 4,000 residents of Tophill were evacuated for 48 hours and a further 4,000 people in the south of the island were cut off for the same period. Captain Mike Lobb RE completed the defusing of the bomb after 32 hours of continuous work.

Small incidents can sometimes bring the unexpected. Sergeant Brian Hodder went to a disturbance caused by a number of 15 year olds having a party while their parents were out for the night. Alcohol was involved rendering one girl semi-conscious. An ambulance was called, but got stuck on a verge so a second one had to be called. It was at this stage that Sgt Hodder admits he should have realised it was going to be one of those nights. His report continued:

'I was informed by youngsters at the scene that the son of the

A Vauxhall Carlton patrol car and officers in a nearly deserted Easton, Portland. In 1994 a wartime bomb was discovered in Portland causing a large part of the island to be evacuated.

Chief Constable Dirk Aldous, QPM, MA (Oxon).

householder had gone off into the woods at the rear of the premises on our arrival. Because it wasn't clear how much he had drunk I commenced a search of the woods with PC Ron Osborne and his dog Jake. These woods are on steeply rising ground and thus difficult to search.

There is no street lighting in the village, it was a cloudy night and because of the dense woodland, very dark. After searching unsuccessfully for about 30 minutes we started to make our way back to the house. It was at this point that the battery on Ron's torch ran out. There were no tracks in the wood and to make any progress we had to climb over fallen trees and force our way through undergrowth.

You can imagine my delight when I came up over a bank and through some stinging nettles, on seeing an apparently flat clearing. On stepping into the clearing I discovered that it was in fact a weed covered pond of stagnant water some three feet deep. I am informed by Ron Osborne that the tucked pike with half twist dive that I performed was worthy of note, but the cleanness of entry into the water left much to be desired. At this point, as though sitting in freezing cold water, with it lapping under my chin, wasn't enough, police dog Jake, a new convert to water sports, decided to join me in the water. I was disappointed in the lack of control that his hysterical handler had over him, this meant that I had to lift the dog out of the water before I could get out myself.

As a result of this unexpected midnight swim I lost my Arnold Baton (truncheon) in the water and despite a search could not find it. I requested that a replacement baton be issued.'

At the end of 1994 Brian Weight retired as Chief Constable, to be replaced by Dirk Aldous, previously Assistant Chief Constable of Hampshire and Deputy Chief Constable of Wiltshire. Before retiring, Brian Weight recalled that when he started his career in Reading 'crime was almost non-existent, an assault on a police officer a rare occurrence – perhaps because it almost certainly carried a six month prison sentence. The last murder in Reading had occurred nearly 20 years previously and drugs were unknown. If a murder did take place one of the 'Big Five' detective chief superintendents from Scotland Yard was sent out to investigate. It was extremely unusual for uniformed constables to deal with a crime. Whereas in 1994, in Dorset, there is at least one firearms incident each week, at least 50,000 other crimes per annum and a growing trend of aggressive youths and the insidious infiltration of drugs.'

Another sign of changing times was the investigation of a paedophile ring in Bournemouth. Operation Meridian became the largest enquiry of its kind ever undertaken in the county. Five men were convicted and sentenced to a total of 51 years imprisonment.

The Child Protection Unit, set up in 1991, was put forward as a model for all to follow. To put children at ease a purpose built interview suite, not on police property, was opened at Sturminster Newton. A Weymouth sergeant,

ABOVE In 1998 Mrs Sally Weld launched the third *Alarm*. Built by Aquastar Workboats in Ireland to specifications supplied by the Force, it has a top speed of 28 knots.

BELOW A view of the 'Streetwise' complex in Wallisdown, a 'film set' replica of various buildings and sites of possible danger used to teach children awareness, and now run as a separate charity.

Bernie Macey, also had the young in mind when he devised a campaign to tackle underage drinking entitled 'Do you know where your children are?' Children misbehaving were filmed on a hand-held video camera before being taken home and the video shown to their parents. It generated a great deal of interest, making Sgt Macey a media star for a short time. Even the Home Secretary heard about the scheme and invited Sergeant Macey and PC Withers to the Home Office to discuss the project.

Crimestoppers came to Dorset when the Force joined the organisation. Crimestoppers began in New Mexico in 1976. A young man working in a filling station had been shot and killed during a robbery. As the police had very little information to go on a hotline was set up to receive anonymous information. Within 72 hours information given on the hotline led to the arrest of two suspects. At the same time information about many other crimes was received. The idea was introduced into the United Kingdom in 1988 and adopted by the Community Action Trust. Although adopted in most of the country it had not been possible to introduce it previously in Dorset because many areas had out-of-county telephone codes, making it difficult to route calls to a central location.

Murder convictions where there is no body found are rare, but a second murder conviction in Dorset of this type was obtained in the case of 40 year old Mrs Packman, who had disappeared from her home in Bournemouth in 1985. All attempts to trace her were unsuccessful. Eight years later her husband was arrested in connection with an unrelated insurance fraud. Extensive enquiries were made by Dorset officers in the UK and abroad which culminated in her husband being convicted of her murder at the end of 1996. He was later sentenced to life imprisonment.

The Crime and Disorder Act of 1998 introduced the need for the police to work with local authorities and other agencies and to formulate community safety plans. A good example of this was the Dorset Interactive Safety Centre at Wallisdown. The Centre, later known as 'Streetwise', was opened in December 1998. Almost £1 million was raised or promised by 150 local businesses and statutory agencies. Students, voluntary groups and the community all made a contribution. 'Streetwise', used for everyday safety education, is a purpose built facility in Dominion Road, which includes a high street, shops, offices, a railway track, farmyard, heathland, building site and a full size house. Constable Andy Saunders, the project manager, was recognised for his work in setting up the Centre by being awarded an MBE for his services to crime prevention.

Police officers have to be ready to handle all sorts of situations, including suicide attempts. Sergeant Thomas Murphy and PC Andrew Steel received Royal Humane Society Awards for an incident involving heights. A man was found on the roof of the County Hotel, Bournemouth, sitting on the edge crying hysterically. PC Steel climbed out of a window onto a small ledge, and jumped a four to five foot gap above a 40 foot drop onto the hotel roof whilst Sergeant Murphy obtained a ladder, and in due course the two officers were able to overpower the man.

At the beginning of 1999 the Force formed an Air Support Unit with a MD Explorer helicopter. Fitted with a 30 million candlepower searchlight and video camera, it is able to reach anywhere within the county from Winfrith in 12 minutes. Its main use is search and rescue work, following possible offenders, and ferrying senior fire officers to the scene of serious fires – where its radar is able

Chief Constable Mrs Jane Stichbury CBE, QPM, MA, BA.

The force became airborne in 1999 when an Air Support Unit was formed after the force took delivery of a MD Explorer helicopter. As long back as 1967 an experiment had been carried out involving nine Southern forces as to the usefulness of a helicopter.

to identify 'hot spots'.

Dick Aldous retired as Chief Constable in 1999 and was replaced by Mrs Jane Stichbury. She had served continuously in the Metropolitan Police after entering as a graduate in 1977. In 1982 she had attended the Special Course at the Police Staff College and steadily rose through the ranks until in 1995 she was appointed as Commander (Crime) Central London. Three years later she was promoted to Deputy Assistant Commissioner.

HRH The Princess Royal being greeted by the Western Divisional Commander, Superintendent Malcolm Palmer, before officially opening the new complex at Chafey's Lake, Weymouth, in 2002.

was transformed into the Dorchester Section Station with the majority of the land being sold. The Eastern Division Headquarters in Ferndown was opened in May 2000 by the Duchess of Gloucester. There was another royal visit during the year by the Earl and Countess of Wessex to the Force open day at Winfrith which attracted over 4,000 visitors. The Western Division Headquarters at Weymouth was opened by HRH The Princess Royal two years later in 2002.

Armed officers appeared on the streets of Bournemouth during the party political conference at the BIC after security was stepped up following a bomb threat. Thankfully there were no bombs in Bournemouth but a much older one was found in Corfe Mullen. PC Sean

Armed officers had first appeared on the streets of Bournemouth in 1994 during that year's party political conference held in the town.

A New Century

The 21st century started off quite well. There had been concern that the change from '99 to '00 would cause computer systems to crash but thankfully it proved a false alarm.

The whole of the Force was prepared for the worst as the New Year celebrations approached but were saved by the 'policeman's friend' – rain. In the Western Division only eleven people were arrested while in Poole the biggest disturbance was from the music festival at Poole Stadium, and that only brought in complaints regarding the noise. In the first six hours of the new millennium there were 53 incidents, ranging from drunkenness to road traffic accidents to burglary. One man was arrested for attempted murder, otherwise it was considered a quiet night. In Bournemouth at the pier approach the 'Pure Energy' road show was performing in front of 12,000 people, and apart from bottles being thrown at the stage and at the crowd, the event passed peacefully, altogether there were only 20 people in custody on New Year's morning for drunkenness to aggravated burglary.

The original Constabulary Headquarters in Dorchester

Constable Sean Foden with a 12,500lb 'Tall Boy' bomb found near Corfe Mullen.

Foden, who was called to investigate, found the object to be about 10ft long and 3ft in diameter. He called in the bomb disposal unit from Tidworth who identified it as being a 12,500lb 'Tall Boy' bomb used to destroy German submarine pens during the Second World War, and they in turn contacted the RAF Bomb Disposal Team. When they arrived PC Foden was somewhat surprised when they started undoing the nuts with a hammer and crowbar. Upon enquiring what would happen if they made a mistake the reply was 'You may experience a slight ringing in your ears' followed by 'if they ever find your ears'. After several hours of hammering it luckily turned out to be filled with concrete and was later revealed to have been part of an experiment to discover if bombers were able to carry its weight.

Heavy weights were something DC Graham Stoakes knew something about. He came first in the 100kg class of the National PAA Powerlifting Championship with a squat of 270kg, a bench press of 180kg and dead lift of 282.5kg and also won the 75kg class. Sergeant Becky Riggs also continued to excel, retaining her four world Tae Kwon-Do championships in 2001.

Crime fighting appeared to be getting even more dangerous. Personal issue body armour went on trial with vests fitted with pockets to carry the array of equipment police officers need such as a radio, cuffs, ASP baton and CS spray. PC Sarah Ackerman of the Operational Support Unit took part in the trials and said 'personally, the moment I put it on, it felt particularly comfortable for driving, walking – you name it!'

An operation in Ferndown led by Detective Chief Inspector Phil James came to a successful end after a six month investigation when Robert Dyer was sentenced to 16 years imprisonment. Operation 'Hornbill' started when a blackmail letter intended to extort money from Tesco was left on a copier in a newsagent. A series of threats followed. An elderly couple received an incendiary device in the post, there was a fire in a post box, whilst a claim made that a bomb had been hidden in the garden of a Tesco customer in Ferndown involved hundreds of officers and soldiers in a major search. The people of Ferndown cooperated and accepted the disruptions with good grace.

Another lengthy operation was a four month covert operation by the drugs squad targeting alleged drug dealers in Weymouth and Portland. Of the 32 people arrested 25 were charged, £10,000 worth of controlled drugs were seized equivalent to 1,400 individual heroin deals. Several thousand pounds worth of cash and assets were also seized.

Sergeant Becky Riggs, the World Tae Kwon-Do Champion.

New Appearances

The huge increase in mobile phones (they had increased from 12 million in 1999 to 40 million in 2001) was having an effect on the number of 999 calls. At the scene of a traffic accident, for example, many people ring in on their mobiles to report it. Phones in pockets or bags can accidently ring 999: these, known as silent calls, made up 30% of the 999 calls received each day by British Telecom.

As part of the National Crime Squad, funded by the Home Office, a High Tech Crime Unit, staffed by two officers, was provided in Dorset to deal with Level 2 crime – such things as paedophilia, persons at risk, major crime investigation, computer misuse and initial internet investigations.

In 2001 Community Wardens, supported jointly by the Force and Purbeck District Council, began appearing in Purbeck. Their purpose was to deter anti-social behavior, and their limited powers enabled them for example to issue penalties for dog fouling and litter. They disappeared with the introduction of Police Community Support Officers.

Weymouth Traffic Wardens Malcolm Baldwin and Roz Clarke were among the last wardens employed by Dorset Police before their duties were taken over by the local council.

Another means of offering advice and help has been through a musical called *Trickster*. PC Andy Saunders wrote the script, lyrics and music to target older people who might be possible victims of burglary. The musical was performed by three professional performers and played to over 2,000 people in its first year.

Also out and about were the men and women of the Dorset Safety Camera Partnership, launched in 2002, whose objective was to reduce road deaths and serious injuries by operating fixed speed cameras and mobile cameras. They were met with a similar reception given to police patrols all those years ago when a non-salute from an AA patrolman meant there was a speed cop about.

Along with most of the public services the police were given targets by the Government and had to prove their efficiency by 'performance indicators'. Mrs Stichbury put these in perspective when writing, 'It is worth emphasising the work going on around the Force on a daily basis which does not feature in the many performance indicators and targets we aim to meet. There are countless incidents of assistance provided to people, sometimes in desperate situations, when we as a professional police service are relied upon to provide a prompt and capable response. I have seen it first hand. It is impressive and first class.' The Chief Constable went on to praise the new Major Crime Investigation Team which, within weeks of its establishment, had to deal with seven murders within a few weeks.

The Home Secretary introduced a package called 'Police Reform'. This was a means of rewarding frontline officers more than those officers in backroom posts and removing what was sometimes referred to as perks (such things as plain clothes allowance).

With the spread of CCTV cameras around Dorset the opportunity was taken to beam pictures from town centre cameras and from the Force helicopter to the control room by using a system first used by US Special Forces in Iraq to send back instant pictures to the US Intelligence organisation in Washington. Dorset Police was the first to use the system in the UK. Harry Brightwell, Head of Information Systems said, 'The sophisticated compression system has allowed us to use our existing networks to transmit pictures of high quality.'

Special Constable Sam Coatsworth met Prime Minister Tony Blair when he attended an evening to honour officers who put themselves at risk of death or serious harm. Sam, who was off duty, was in the Sandbanks area near the ferry when he saw a Rolls Royce car shoot forward over the harbour wall down a six foot embankment and into the sea where it started to sink. The vehicle's driver, a 59 year old man, was assisted by another man while Sam tried to help the 74 year old lady passenger who was unable to undo her seat belt and also had her foot trapped. The vehicle was sinking fast and the sea pouring in through the sunroof. Sam climbed onto the bonnet and leaned fully through the sunroof, completely submerging himself. He managed to free the woman's foot, pull her free and carry her to safety. Within a minute the car became totally submerged. Sam also received a Royal Humane Society Award.

In July 2004 Chief Constable Stichbury was appointed one of Her Majesty's Inspector of Constabulary responsible for inspecting the Forces in the Southern Region. In December Martin Baker was appointed Chief Constable. He had joined the Metropolitan Police in 1975 and after serving in West Mercia Constabulary and Gwent

Chief Constable Martin Baker QPM, BSc (Hons), MBA.

The Prince of Wales and Countess of Cornwall with the Chief Constable during their visit to Force Headquarters in 2006.

Police was appointed Assistant Chief Constable and later Deputy Chief Constable in Gloucestershire.

Over the last few years officers from Dorset Police could be found working in many parts of the world. After the 9/11 terrorist incident in New York in 2001 officers were sent to help out as family liaison officers. Others have served in Bosnia, Iraq and in Thailand after the Tsunami in 2004. 2005 saw officers from Dorset policing in Scotland during the G5 Summit and Cardiff for the finance ministers conference. The Force Control Room receives 94,000 emergency 999 calls every year and the casualty bureau is part of a national network that allows it to take calls during crises, such as the London bombings.

The Prince of Wales and the Duchess of Cornwall paid tribute to the Force by visiting the Headquarters in its anniversary year. After visiting the Control Room and casualty bureau, the Prince said. 'I often think that we take so easily for granted the amazing work our police forces do, so often unseen and unheard . . . we are incredibly fortunate in this country with the police forces we have.'

Britain has been described as a more vulgar and

The high-speed police rib can operate in the shallow waters of Poole Harbour

The modern Control Room at the Winfrith Headquarters of Dorset Police.

aggressive nation – there has been a tenfold increase in violent crime since 1979. The public's main concern though, remains that of anti-social behaviour – but in this regard, some things never seem to change. In 1857, the year after the formation of the Dorset Constabulary, this article appeared in a local Sherborne newspaper: 'One of those nuisances termed 'skimington riding' was concocted last week by some idle fellows, who proceeded round town with a couple of effigies, yelling and shouting, and causing great uproar. Just as they arrived at the Conduit one of their ringleaders was suddenly pounced upon by the police and borne off to the lock up. We are very pleased with this, the first sally of the new police, for we hope it indicates that they are strictly instructed to keep order in our streets, and we hope to find them following up this step by clearing the pavements, the churchyard and other places of disorderly boys, especially on Sundays.'

Whatever the future may bring to the Dorset Police, its officers will still be on duty 24 hours a day, doing their best to keep order on Dorset's streets and upholding the law just as their predecessors endeavoured to do throughout the last 150 years.

150 years after its creation in 1856, the principal duties and function of the Dorset Police remain largely unchanged. Here two officers are patrolling the Great Dorset Steam Rally. The event attracts thousands of people and despite being the modern equivalent of the Victorian Woodbury Hill Fair it causes far less trouble.

Dorset Police is organised into four territorial divisions. The boroughs of Poole and Bournemouth each have a division based on their local government area. The rest of the county is divided into two divisions – East and West – with their headquarters at Ferndown and Weymouth respectively. There are also administrative divisions and departments at the Force Headquarters, Winfrith, such as the Operations Division (responsible for among others, traffic, air support, dogs and the marine section) and the Headquarters CID. The strength of the Force is made up of 1,482 police officers, 1,133 police staff, 250 special constables and 83 volunteers.

Appendix

CHIEF CONSTABLES

Lt Colonel S.S. Cox	1856 – 1867
Captain Amyatt Brown	1867 – 1898
Captain Dennis Granville	1898 – 1924
Major Lionel W. Peel Yates, KPM	1924 – 1955
Lt Colonel Ronald B. Greenwood OBE KPM	1955 – 1961
Arthur Hambleton, Esq CBE MC QPM DL	1962 – 1980
David Owen, Esq QPM	1980 – 1982
Brian Weight, Esq QPM	1982 – 1994
Dirk Aldous, Esq QPM MA(Oxon)	1994 – 1999
Mrs Jane Stichbury CBE QPM BA MA	1999 – 2004
Martin Baker, Esq QPM BSc MBA	2005 –

CLERKS OF THE PEACE AND OF THE POLICE AUTHORITY

W. Ffooks, Esq	1856 – 1872
T. Ffooks, Esq	1872 – 1889
E.A. Ffooks, Esq	1889 – 1925
J.L. Torr, Esq	1926 – 1935
C.P. Brutton, Esq, CBE	1935 – 1961
T.J.W. Templeman CBE	1961 – 1967
K.A. Abel, Esq, CBE DL	1967 – 1991
P.K. Harvey, Esq, LLB DL	1991 – 2006
M. Goscomb, Esq	2006 –

CHAIRMEN OF THE POLICE COMMITTEE OF QUARTER SESSIONS

Henry Frampton, Esq	1856 – 1878
Bendall Littlehales, Esq	1878 – 1880
Lt Colonel George P. Mansel	1881
Carr Stuart Glyn, Esq	1882
Lt Colonel George P. Mansel	1883 – 1889

CHAIRMEN OF THE STANDING JOINT COMMITTEE

Lt Colonel George P. Mansel	1889 – 1893
H.B. Middleton, Esq	1893 – 1916
Colonel J.R.P. Goodden, OBE	1916 – 1922
Colonel R.H. Simonds, OBE	1922 – 1924
Colonel T.A. Colfox	1924 – 1933
A.J. Woodroffe, Esq MBE	1933 – 1951
Captain A.V. Hambro, DL	1951 – 1953
Captain H. Kirby	1953 – 1960

CHAIRMEN OF POLICE COMMITTEES

Colonel Sir Joseph Weld, OBE TD	1960 – 1980
Major General Mark Bond	1980 – 1992
Sir Stephen Hammick	1992 – 1996
Peter Jones, Esq	1996 – 2003
Michael G. Taylor, Esq CBE	2003 –

AWARDS AND HONOURS

Superintendent S. Lovell	MBE	1927
Assistant Chief Constable Harry Lovell	KPM	1951
Chief Constable Major Peel Yates	KPM	1952
Superintendent Frank Elmes	QPM	1956
Constable Cornick	BEM	1956
Constable Kenneth Pearce	BEM	1965
Chief Constable Arthur Hambleton	QPM	1966
" "	OBE	1971
" "	DL	1978
" "	CBE	1977
Sergeant Derrick Highmore	BEM	1975
Constable Drew	QGM	1979
Sergeant Stroud	QCBC	1979
Chief Constable David Owen	QPM	1981
Constable John Howes	BEM	1981
Constable Gerry Elkins	BEM	1985
Inspector Tony Hutley	QPM	1987
Superintendent Gerry Needham	QPM	1987
Detective Sergeant Philip Drake	BEM	1990
Assistant Chief Constable Alan Rose	QPM	1991
Superintendent Julia Lunn	MBE	1991
Ex Superintendent Len Chick	MBE	1991
Inspector Andy Mason, Constables Elsdon, Harris, Lavin and Hester	QCBC	1993
Deputy Chief Constable Tony Pointer	QPM	1993
Assistant Chief Constable Sue Davies	QPM	1993
Constable Derek Watton	BEM	1993
Chief Commandant Bob Short	MBE	1994
Chief Constable Dirk Aldous	QPM	1995
Detective Chief Superintendent Des Donohoe	QPM	1997
Divisional Commandant Pauline Edwards	MBE	1997
Chief Constable Brian Weight	QPM	1999
Deputy Chief Constable Andy May	QPM	1999
Constable Andy Saunders	MBE	2000
Chief Constable Jane Stichbury	QPM	2000
	CBE	2004
Constable Brenda Traylen	MBE	2004
Chief Constable Martin Baker	QPM	2006

QGM = Queen's Gallantry Medal

QCBC = Queen's Commendation for Brave Conduct

Acknowledgements

I wish to acknowledge the work of Jack Gray and Miss D. Holmes in producing the centenary history in 1956, without which the task of writing this book would have been so much more difficult. I thank also all those who contributed knowingly or unknowingly by recording their experiences and memories for our pleasure and education. I wish also to acknowledge those who are not mentioned anywhere but have served loyally and contributed equally to the story of policing in Dorset.

My thanks go to my work colleagues for answering the many questions I have put to them and for putting up with me when my mind has been absent without leave! That goes especially for Alison who has heard more about past times than sometimes she would have wished. I thank the Chief Constable and Force for allowing me to produce this book and David Burnett for contributing much more than is expected of a publisher.